THERE IS POWER
IN THE SPOKEN
WORD OF GOD

GLADYS CONTEH

WESTBOW
PRESS®
A DIVISION OF THOMAS NELSON
& ZONDERVAN

WestBow Press books may be ordered through booksellers or by contacting:

WestBow Press
A Division of Thomas Nelson & Zondervan
1663 Liberty Drive
Bloomington, IN 47403
www.westbowpress.com
844-714-3454

ISBN: 978-1-6642-3421-5 (sc)
ISBN: 978-1-6642-3423-9 (hc)
ISBN: 978-1-6642-3422-2 (e)

Library of Congress Control Number: 2021909623

Print information available on the last page.

WestBow Press rev. date: 05/20/2021

DEDICATION

This book is dedicated to the Lord God for enabling me to share my experiences and walk with Him. For with Him, all things are possible; with Him, nothing is too difficult or too far gone, to them that believe!

And,
I thank my beloved husband, John and our boys, Jesse, Josh, Jermaine, Jadon, and Jason for their tremendous and continuous care, support, and encouragement throughout the years!
To Christ Jesus be all the glory!

NOTE FROM THE AUTHOR

I am a child of God, who loves the Lord Jesus Christ with every fiber of my being and wants to share my experiences of the Lord with others, through the power of the Holy Spirit at work in me. My entire life is a living testimony of the love, power, and faithfulness of the Lord Jesus through His unchanging and powerful Word.

To God be all the glory!

As the rain and the snow come down from heaven, and do not return to it without watering the earth and making it bud and flourish, so that it yields seed for the sower and bread for the eater, so is My word that goes out from My mouth: it will not return to Me empty but will accomplish what I desire and achieve the purpose for which I sent it. (Isaiah 55:10–11 NIV).

CONTENTS

INTRODUCTION

There is power in the spoken Word of God (the Bible or Scriptures)—supernatural power in the spoken Word of God! God is all powerful, and with infinite power over all created things! Therefore, every spoken or written Word of God is firm because it has already come to pass—that is why it was written. The Word of God tells us that everything was created through the spoken Word or command of God. He commanded everything into being from things that were not seen. We were also created in the image and likeness of the almighty God, a resemblance of the Father. Therefore, a person is not limited by anything or anyone, but limited by who they are in Christ Jesus, their knowledge of God, and their faith in the Lord Jesus. Declare what the Word of God says in every circumstance, believing that whatever you ask for in prayer, according to His Word, you receive them, and you shall have them. If you can believe it, you can have it according to His Word, because faith is understanding God, His Word, and His ways. Believe and declare, according to the Word of God what you want to see happen in your life, and not what you have, feel, or know. Whatever emanates out of your mouth comes out of the abundance of your heart and it determines your fate as a child of God, because your heart is in tune with God's heart. The way one thinks comes from their belief, and this will reflect in the words declared. What you declare has the power of life and death—the power to make or break. While on earth, Christ Jesus spoke to every situation; just a word from Him changed every circumstance.

Remember, God is not a genie in a bottle!—He never responds to man's demands just to prove Himself. God is who He is: unchanging, sovereign, almighty, all powerful, immortal, invisible, faithful, and just. There must be a relationship with God through His Son Jesus Christ our Lord; there must be a longing after His Heart, to know and serve Him according to His Word. Christ Jesus is the image of the invisible God, complete with all the fullness of the Father, who came in the flesh and reconciled man back unto the Father. No one can reach the Father, except through the Son. Christ Jesus, the living Word is proven to be true as He was tried, tested and purified. We must believe in Him and receive His gift of salvation because He has loved us with an everlasting love. Love is the foundation of the Father, and upon which everything is built; God is love! God is seeking worshippers that will worship and have a true spiritual relationship with Him because of who He is. The Father desires true worship that is beyond measure—a worship based on our love for Him (crazy kind of love, the love of Christ in our hearts). The Father's utmost desire is that we become more like Him in every way. If you earnestly believe in and understand the life changing Word of God with every fiber of your being, then you can have whatever you truly believe according to His will, without a shadow of doubt. God is faithful to every Word He has spoken; He cannot deny Himself. Faith, like love, is the centerpiece of our relationship with God our Father; we must have faith to start a true spiritual relationship with Him. Faith is a living thing because it is alive and active, and one must activate it to start a relationship with the Lord God. Faith sees beyond what our naked eyes perceive; it gives supernatural confidence in God and His Word. If you remain in the Lord Jesus, and His Word remains in you, whatever you ask according to His Word, will be done for you through the power of the Holy Spirit.

The leadership of the Holy Spirit brings every spoken Word to pass, and it is the 'pattern' or 'blueprint' God has set for His church or children since the day of Pentecost. Without the Holy Spirit there is no true church, no true relationship, and the worship of God becomes nothing but dead worship (without power). God cannot work through the dead but via the living in the power of His Spirit. It is only the Spirit of God that reveals the things of God and knows the mind of God because God is a Spirit. Relationship with the Holy Spirit leads us to a willing and obedient heart. God can do anything and everything we cannot do; we are nothing, but He is everything good we ought to be. His glory, love, and character exist in everything He has created in us and around us. We must align ourselves with the Word of God and believe in the Lord Jesus Christ and His Holy Spirit; only then, can we realize our identity and potential. God is still looking for a genuine relationship with us, a relationship wherein mankind is more like Him, and live according to His Holy Word. In other words, God wants us to be a new creation, born of His Spirit. When our eyes are poised on the master and walking in His will for our lives, every Word of God that we declare in the mighty name of Jesus Christ will surely come to pass. If we see with the eyes of God, see what God sees with the eyes of faith that call things that are not as though they were, then the master creator, the Elshaddai, the great physician, and the almighty, is ready to perform whatever He has promised in His Word. See victory and declare it! It is about time the children of God stand up for the truth. No more excuses!

This book is a collection of messages or food as I call it from the Lord, that my family and I have written and fed on over the years in Him, through the power of His Holy Spirit. This spiritual food has strengthened, refreshed, and renewed our minds, souls, spirits, and our work with the Lord. Hence, has drawn us closer to a deeper, eternal, and true spiritual relationship with the Lord Jesus Christ our savior. God's Word and His glory given to us cannot just be contained within us, because we are only vessels unto Him. He has given it for the world, for the salvation and refreshing of *all* who accept it. Thus, I want others to experience this same true love relationship with the Father through the power of His Spirit, which is the motivation for this book; for the many out there, who are hungry for the living God and His Word. As you read this book, my earnest prayer is that you have a personal encounter with the Lord Jesus Christ, whereby something changes on the inside out. May the Lord Jesus Christ enlighten the eyes of your understanding through the power of His Holy Spirit, so that you will comprehend the full revelation of who He is, His divine love, His truth, His glory, and the power of His resurrection. May you also fall in love with Him leading to an eternal true relationship like I have; and may His love in you stems in every area of your life, all to His glorious and divine pleasure. And may the words of your mouth and the meditations of your heart be in line with God's unchanging Word, and be pleasing in His sight, through Christ Jesus our Lord. Amen!

1

THE SOVEREIGNTY OF GOD

The Lord God is the sovereign God, the everlasting God, and the creator of the ends of the earth. He is the Lord, and apart from Him there is no savior; from ancient of days, He is, and forever He will be. He is the first and the last, the beginner, the end, and the finisher of all things. In His wrath, no one can deliver from His hand; when He acts, who can reverse it? His own hands laid the foundations of the earth, and His right hand spreads out the heavens like a canopy. It is He who brings out the starry host one by one and call them by name; because of His great power and mighty strength, not one of them is missing. He is the omnipotent God who is all knowing, all wise; the omniscient God who is all seeing—nothing is hidden from His eyes. The omnipresent God who is all present, is capable of being everywhere at the same time, and His divine presence encompasses the whole universe. He is the almighty, all powerful, and holy God, whose understanding is unsearchable, and His thoughts and ways are higher than ours. The Lord deserves our praise, worship, and adoration for great is His name! He is the king eternal, the immortal, the invisible God, who alone is wise, the almighty—to Him be all glory and honor forever and ever.

Amen. He measured the waters in the hollow of His hands and the heavens with a span and calculated the dust of the earth. He weighed the mountains in scales and the hills in a balance. Who has ever directed the Spirit of the Lord or taught Him as His counselor? With whom did He take counsel, or who has taught Him in the path of justice, knowledge, or understanding? The nations are as a drop in a bucket, counted as the small drop on the scale (Isaiah 40 NKJV). Who is like our God, to whom will you liken Him, or to whom will you compare Him? Or who is His equal? All nations are as *nothing* before Him and are counted by Him *less than nothing and worthless*. God is a way maker where there is no way; He divided the Red Sea for His people to cross through (Exodus 14 NKJV). He provided bread (manna) from heaven for the Israelites in the wilderness; man ate the bread of angels. What a mighty God we serve! He is who He says He is; the unchanging God, a covenant keeper, and faithful to every word He has said. He is not a man that He should lie or change His mind, neither does He promise and not fulfill them (Numbers 23:19 NIV).

God is all powerful, and with infinite power over all created things! The God who has numbered every string of hair on your head and knows which one falls is Lord of *all*. He knows our tomorrow and owns our next breath. Without Him we can do or be nothing because in Him we live, in Him we move, and in Him we have our being (Acts 17:28 NKJV). You were created in His image and likeness, with a specific purpose that only you can fulfill. He chose you and formed you for a set purpose, so seek Him with every fiber of your being in order to fulfill that reason for which He has wonderfully and perfectly created you. Is anything too hard for the Lord? Nothing is too hard for the Lord (Genesis 18:14 NIV). "My people are destroyed for lack of knowledge." (Hosea 4:6 NKJV). Lack of the knowledge and understanding of who God is and His ways. Hence, let us pursue the Lord while He may be found; forsake our old ways, surrender, and trust in Him. He will give us peace, the peace that surpasses all human knowledge and understanding. Fear not, dear friends, for He has called you by His name, created you for His glory, formed you with His righteous hands and yes, made you to be partakers of His salvation and glory. There is nothing too difficult for the Lord—the one who sits above the circle of the earth, and His inhabitants are like grasshoppers. He who stretches out the heavens like a curtain, and spreads them out like a tent to dwell in. He sets up princes and brings them to nothing and makes the judges of the earth useless. The Lord God created all things; He spread forth the earth and that which comes from it. He gives breath to the people and spirit to those who walk on the earth. The Lord is His name, and His glory and praise He will not give to another. The Lord is worthy of our praise, and His Word will *never* fail; it stands forever.

One day as I was on my way to work, the Lord gave me this word that, "It does not matter what people think or believe about Him because it does not change who He is or what He has done." In other words, God is sovereign over *all* things—in heaven, on earth, and under the earth, visible and invisible things; He is the creator and sustainer of everything then, now, and forevermore. Whether people want to believe in God or not, it does not matter or change Him at all; but it matters all the most to people. Human beliefs about God do not change who He is or what He has done. He is still who He is—God, and creator of all things, and forever He will be. And that is a *fact*! The things the Lord God has put in place from the time of creation even to now still stand! The sun shines for both the wicked and the righteous, the rain and snow come down at their appointed time, seasons change, humans, creatures, and other living things are still reproducing after their kind. The Lord, our God almighty, changes not. His character, nature, glory, ways, word, and splendor remain the same and fill the heavens and the earth. As the psalmist says:

The heavens declare the glory of God; the skies proclaim the work of His hands. Day after day they pour forth speech; night after night they reveal knowledge. They have no speech; they use no words; and no sound is heard from them. Yet their voice goes out into all the earth, their words to the ends of the world. (Psalms 19:1–4 NIV).

To God be all the glory, honor, and praise! He is worthy of our praise. Now, let us look at some key Messages and Food from the Lord about His sovereignty and awe.

THE GLORY OF GOD

When we talk about the glory of God, we think about all that God is—His nature, character, and ways that make Him who He is. It is fundamental as children of God to have a clear knowledge of God because knowledge leads to understanding. When you have the full revelation of God through Christ Jesus, your perception changes; as each person's perception of God is based on their knowledge of Him. One's knowledge of God leads to understanding of Him (His character, nature and ways), and understanding leads to reverential fear, love, and obedience. One cannot understand God or even have a true spiritual relationship with Him without knowing Him. King Solomon in the book of Proverbs reminds us that, "The fear of the LORD is the beginning of wisdom, and the knowledge of the Holy One is understanding." (Proverbs 9:10 NIV). This knowledge starts with, who God is—God's immeasurable glory. Let us start by looking at what God's glory is in the first place. The Hebrew word most used for glory is "kabowd," which means "weight, in a good sense; splendor, great brightness, magnificence, parade, pomp, brilliance and abundance or plentiful, abounding in words, exuberant" (Concordance). And the Greek word most used is "doxa," which means dignity, honor, praise, and worship. It suggests reputation such as what one thinks of another (Concordance). From these definitions, it becomes clear that God's glory is something that is infinite or immeasurable in its magnitude, power, wisdom and splendor; it is astounding in appearance that will only lead to an impulsive submission of praise and worship before His presence (His nature or inherent glory). However, it is more than that; God's glory is not just His splendor, magnificent or brilliance, but it is also in His reputation, His revealed character—the display of His attributes. Throughout the entire Word of God or the Bible, every time God revealed His intrinsic glory or radiance of His being, the men of God or prophets fell facedown as though dead in awe of His magnificent presence. For example, the prophet Ezekiel saw the inherent glory of God in the book of Ezekiel, the first chapter, when he was by the Kebar River in the land of the Babylonians (modern-day Iraq). There, the Spirit of the Lord was upon him and he saw visions of God—yes, visions—that terrified him greatly because of the power displayed in the glory of God. Here is how the prophet described his experience:

> Above the vault over their heads was what looked like a throne of lapis lazuli, and high above on the throne was a figure like that of a man. I saw that from what appeared to be His waist up He looked like glowing metal, as if full of fire, and that from there down He looked like fire; and brilliant light surrounded Him. Like the appearance of a rainbow in the clouds on a rainy day, so was the radiance around Him. This was the appearance of the likeness of the glory of the LORD. When I saw it, I fell facedown, and I heard the voice of one speaking. (Ezekiel 1:26–28 NIV).

No one can withstand the radiance of the glory of the Lord God; it brings about awe, reverential fear, and worship before His presence—it produces total surrender in fear of His greatness.

Again, when Moses asked God to show him His glory, He said to him:

> I will cause all My goodness to pass in front of you, and I will proclaim My name, the LORD, in your presence. I will have mercy on whom I will have mercy, and I will have compassion on whom I will have compassion. But, He said, you cannot see My face, for no one may see Me and live. (Exodus 33:19–20 NIV).

God could only reveal His character and goodness (merciful, compassionate, gracious, slow to anger, abounding in love, faithful, forgiving, and just) to Moses, but not His entire splendor or magnificence to him because no one could withstand such a sight—the brilliance or brightness of His face. It is simply unfathomable to see that God could respond in such a way and manifest His presence before a man who asked for it. The Bible says that God made all His goodness pass before Moses, even though, He would not allow Moses to see His face. On that day, Moses experienced the tangible, touchable, or physical presence of the living God. To glorify God then, is to increase His reputation by revealing His true nature and character and living according to the fruit of His Spirit in you. "But the fruit of the Spirit is love, joy, peace, longsuffering, kindness, goodness, faithfulness, gentleness, and self-control. Against such things there is no law." (Galatians 5:22 NIV). This is what the world must see through the church, through the life of the believer or God's children in Christ Jesus.

As stated, God's inherent glory is the glory that is infinite or immeasurable in its greatness, brilliance, and magnificence by who God is. We could say then because of who God is—*He is glorious, and that His glory separates Him from all other created beings.* In order words, *God's glory is all that He is.* When God's magnificent or wonderful splendor is manifested before us, we are in the presence not only of God, but of all that He is. God is inherently and infinitely glorious and His person will never be changed by time or location. When God lived between the cherubim in the ark of the covenant in Moses' tabernacle, His displayed glory was as real as it is today in heaven. God cannot diminish or moderate or reduce Himself in any way to accommodate any person. This is an important principle to learn and if we understand it, we will realize that God wants us to change to accommodate Him. We cannot ask God to change to accommodate us. If we did, we would be asking Him to decrease His glory, decrease His person and stand down from being infinite, and from every attribute. If God could tone down His glory to accommodate us, He would be asked to do it with His love and holiness. It is impossible to comprehend or realize the magnificence of God, or even imagine it, but it does exist and let it suffice or suit us to say that God is glorious in every way and in everything He had created. Even Moses experienced the inherent or innate glory of God. God also proclaimed His name before Moses—the name of the Lord (Jehovah), declares that He is. His name is all encompassing, and when spoken out of the mouth of God Himself, it is the most powerful word that any of the Old Testament saints could ever have heard or perceived. *When God speaks His own powerful name, there is nothing left to say, and there is nothing anyone could add to it. It simply defines all that God is.* Moses not only experienced God's physical presence, but also His spiritual presence when God spoke, because God's word is Spirit. How much more spiritually powerful could anyone be than to hear God Himself speak His own name.

God's glory is God's best, it is all that He is. When God's glory is manifested in our presence, we do not have a type of God in our midst, or a facet or surface or side of God in our midst, but rather *all* of God with *all* His infinite attributes. As believers, we have the potential to display these attributes because we have the indwelling presence of the Holy Spirit. You see, God did what a human asked, He displayed His best. Likewise, God would want people to also display their best. Why? Because we are in covenant with Him. God wants us to display all of Him; we must endeavor to reveal Jesus Christ in all His splendor.

When the glory of God is in our midst friends, we do not only have God in our midst, but we have God speaking in our midst. This is still the way in which God operates today. He has come into our midst (in the flesh) and now He speaks to us through the Holy Spirit. God has not only displayed His glory in our midst, but He has also come in His fullness to reside permanently in the heart of the believer, so He can communicate and fellowship with us. We can never be the same when we understand this. Be strong in the power of God's might even as you display God's intrinsic and ascribed glory through His spoken word in the mighty name of Jesus Christ! Amen.

GOD'S ASCRIBED GLORY

God's glory is not limited to His infinite nature and character, it also includes His *ascribed glory,* which is the result of His inherent glory. When we talk about God's ascribed glory, we are looking at the appreciation and acknowledgement of all that the sovereign God is—His attributes, which includes His inherent splendor or radiance (Concordance). *Ascribed glory is our gratitude and thankfulness to God for all that He is.* This majestic glory of the Lord God only leads to a total surrender of praise and worship of Him. Praise and worship are vehicles through which we glorify God, and the substance behind our praise is God's glory. Since praise is a journey and lifestyle, then our lifestyle is one vehicle through which we glorify God. As we stated before, when the glory of God is in our midst friends, we not only have God in our midst, but we have God speaking and moving in our midst. We must ascribe God's glory through our reverential fear of Him, which leads us into praise and worship; we must recognize and acknowledge who God is and all that He has done in every area of our lives. Let us talk about God's sovereignty and power in every situation or circumstance when we do not know which way to go, when all hopes are gone, or have received a bad report. Let us talk about Christ Jesus, through His Word, as we wait on Him because He is greater than anything including problems or challenges, we would ever face. *He is from above and above all.* God has not only displayed His glory in our midst, but He has also come in His fullness to reside permanently in the heart of the believer through His Holy Spirit, so He can communicate and fellowship with us forever. We know that we cannot give God any strength or add to His glory in any way, but we can acknowledge it and tell everyone about it—for this very reason we were created. If God's glory is all that He is, then we are created to the praise of His glory. Not only in everything we do, but in everything we are, and should be, to the praise of His glory. The obvious distinction is that the believer will glorify God and the unbeliever will not. If the believer does not glorify God in his/her lifestyle, it is because his/her lifestyle is not right. The believer's lifestyle should glorify God through his/her actions; and these actions will be very strongly centered around worship. A lifestyle of worship demonstration will reveal God's glory, and this glory is most effectively displayed through lifestyle.

There is a distinction between the Old Testament saints and the New Testament saints in this regard—the Old Testament saints glorified God by praising His attributes, they saw God as a separated being, and they were very much aware of the fact that they were created to praise the creator. Now God continues to display Himself to people, but He does it through person to person. We see God in each other, and the world sees God in us;

God is no longer separated from humans, and we do not have to look for God outside of ourselves. Thus, the New Testament saints glorify God by living His attributes, a display case of God's life and nature. God has chosen it to be this way. "And the Word became flesh and dwelt among us, and we beheld His glory, the glory as of the only begotten of the Father, full of grace and truth." (John 1:14 NKJV). Remember, we are in a covenant with the Father through Christ Jesus, and God's Word is no longer only God's, but it is also yours and mine. We are supposed to live it because we are Godlike, or more specifically, Christlike. Our Lord Jesus Christ had to live the words He spoke; otherwise, His disciples and the people around Him would have never seen God. When the Word became flesh, it had to be lived. Glorifying God is allowing the Word to be manifested through us. The revealed character or displayed attributes of God are no longer just with God but have been given to humans; and these attributes are the fruits of the Spirit. God's glory cannot be contained within anointed earthly vessels; it is for the world—for the salvation of people. The world waits earnestly with bated breath for the glory of God to be manifested through His children. When you fill your home and life with praise; everything around you will be subjected to the Spirit of God in you. In praise and worship, we proclaim that this world is not all that there is, and the inhabitants are subject to a higher authority. As we glorify God, we overcome and defeat the powers of darkness that surround and try to influence us. Paul teaches us that, Christ has disarmed these powers. Praise and worship enact this victory and celebrate it; it neutralizes the powers that are against us and sets the stage for the manifestation of God's glory on the earth. The prelude to this manifestation will be a tremendous manifestation of God's praises. Praise will lay the foundation for God's glory to shine universally. So, let us ascribe glory to God, for He has done great things!

ASCRIBE GREATNESS TO
THE LORD OUR GOD!

"For I proclaim the name of the LORD: Ascribe greatness to our God. He is the Rock, His work is perfect; for all His ways are justice, a God of truth and without injustice; righteous and upright is He." (Deuteronomy 32: 3–4 NKJV). God is worthy of our praise because He is our solid rock (unshakeable), the truth, the righteous, and the upright; His work and ways are perfect, just, and without discrimination. He has loved us with an everlasting love; the love that God has for us is something we should use as a foundation for all our praise and adoration. Let us be intentional in giving God the glory that is due to His name through our fellowship and relationship with Him. As declared before, praise is the reality of the Word of God working in and through us. A lifestyle of praise and worship is the result of constantly believing and appreciating God, and His Word. The book of Psalms is a collection of songs of praises to God; and here is a couple of Psalms by King David. King David wrote a song of praise for the Lord's faithfulness to His people:

> Make a joyful shout to the LORD, all you lands!
> Serve the LORD with gladness; Come before His
> presence with singing. Know that the LORD,
> He is God; it is He who has made us, and not we
> ourselves; we are His people and the sheep of His
> pasture. Enter His gates with thanksgiving, and
> into His courts with praise. Be thankful to Him,
> and bless His name. For the LORD is good; His
> mercy is everlasting, and His truth endures to all
> generations. (Psalms 100:1–5 NKJV).

Oh, sing to the LORD a new song! For He has done marvelous things; His right hand and His holy arm have gained Him the victory. The LORD has made known His salvation; His righteousness He has revealed in the sight of the nations. He has remembered His mercy and His faithfulness to the house of Israel; all the ends of the earth have seen the salvation of our God. Shout joyfully to the LORD, all the earth; break forth in song, rejoice, and sing praises. Sing to the LORD with the harp, With the harp and the sound of a psalm, with trumpets and the sound of a horn, shout joyfully before the LORD, the King. Let the sea roar, and all its fullness, the world and those who dwell in it; let the rivers clap their hands; let the hills be joyful together before the LORD, for He is coming to judge the earth. With righteousness, He shall judge the world, and the peoples with equity. (Psalms 98:1–9 NKJV).

We have every reason to ascribe glory to the Lord our God and give Him the praise due to His name, for He is worthy to be praised. Declare the Word of God to what you want to see happen and not what you have because of the power in the spoken Word of God! God is unfathomable and so are all His ways!

THE UNFATHOMABLE GOD AND HIS LOVE FOR US

A lot of times, we tend to forget how great, powerful, faithful, and wonderful our Lord God is. *We need to know that this unfathomable God we serve is not a God made by human hands, but the God who created all things out of things that were not seen. He owns it all—all things in heaven and on earth and under the earth, visible and invisible, thrones, dominion, and powers. All things were created by Him and for Him; all things originate with Him and come from Him and live through*

Him. This is the God whom we serve, and He lives in us through His Holy Spirit when we accept His sacrificial atonement for us on the cross of calvary—Christ Jesus our Lord. Each day, I am overwhelmed by the greatness of our God through everything around us; from the tiniest things that we take for granted to the mightiest things that we perceive as too big for God to handle. Yet He shows Himself mighty, faithful, and above every condition or problem. Nothing is too hard or difficult for the Lord God, the creator and sustainer of all things. Just abide in the Lord and in His Word and you shall experience His glory and goodness in every way because He is faithful.

The apostle Paul, filled with the Holy Spirit, talked about the wisdom and knowledge of God; how unfathomable, inscrutable, and unsearchable are His judgments. How untraceable, mysterious and undiscoverable are His ways, plans, paths, or methods (Romans 11:33 NIV). Whenever you forget about the greatness or power of God, just go back to the Old Testament to reflect on the ways and acts of our God among His people—the Israelites, whom He chose to reveal Himself to, as God. These books of the Old Testament are the foundation upon which Christianity was built; it was as a result, the handbook of the early Christians. Christ Jesus is the fulfillment of everything God talked about and promised in the Old Testament. Your very existence is a miracle from God, and when you become overwhelmed by the greatness and awesomeness of our God and His love for us, everything becomes small or nothing in the presence of God. Know that it is from God and through Him all things exist, and there is none like Him; He is above all things, and in Him all things hold together. Without Him, we can do nothing because His breath is in us; and in Him we live, move and have our being.

The mysteries and secrets of God no man can understand; the hidden things of God, His plans, His works, His love, His grace, and mercy, humans cannot understand or comprehend in our finite or limited minds. Only the Spirit of God can reveal to us the deep things of God. Apostle Paul mentioned in 1 Corinthians that, "However, as it is written: What no eye has seen, what no ear has heard, and what no human mind has conceived—the things that God has prepared for those that love Him—these are the things God has revealed to us by His Spirit. The Holy Spirit of God searches all things, even the deep things of God." (1 Corinthians 2:9–10 NIV). It is only through the power of the Holy Spirit that we can understand the will, plan or ways of God. *Without the Holy Spirit, there is no Christianity,* and *no* true worship of the Father, because God is a Spirit, and it takes His Spirit to reveal to us His mind and ways. Hence, God's true worshippers must worship in spirit and in truth (according to the Word of God). We must understand the immeasurable, unlimited, and surpassing greatness of the power of the Holy Spirit in us and for us that believe in the Lord Jesus Christ. God is alive, and He is always at work all over the world through His Holy Spirit in the name of Jesus Christ.

The Word of God tells us in the book of Proverbs, the first chapter and the seventh verse that, "The fear of the Lord is the beginning of knowledge, but fools despise wisdom and instruction." (Proverbs 1:7 NIV). We must have a reverential fear of God and be overwhelmed by who He is and what He has done through Christ Jesus. Seek to know Him more and more each day, so that you will please Him in every way. *God is who He says He is, He will do what He says He will do because He is His Word; He is faithful and cannot deny Himself.* He is the beginning of all things and surely the end of all things. Endeavour to have a spiritual relationship with the Lord more and more, so that you can serve Him better even leading into eternity. Remember that everything will pass away, but God and His Word will remain; whatever He has said in His Word stands, not because of you or me but because of who He is and what He has done. If God said it in His Word, then that confirms its validity; speak His Word in faith without wavering because there is power in the spoken Word of God!

BLESS THE LORD O MY SOUL

David loved the Lord, and he had the revelation of who God is; he was a man after God's heart, and he wanted to please God in every way. We could see that David was commanding his soul to bless the Lord God almighty, who is worthy of all praise. The word "bless" in Hebrew is "barak:" to "bow down, to kneel, to praise." (Concordance). This was an act of humility, affection, adoration, and gratitude towards the supreme and eternal creator of all. David was surrendering all of himself, even the deepest part of his being—his soul. The word "soul" in Hebrew is "nephesh:" "breathing creature" (Concordance). David saw himself as nothing but a mere breathing creature; like any other creature (nothing of importance before the Lord God). Likewise, my friends, we are nothing, but mere breathing creatures created to give God all the praise and glory. So, always declare God's Word with confidence and awe.

The human soul is always in contrary to the Spirit, (wanting to go his or her own way); the soul is that part of us that controls our emotions, feelings, thoughts, and the mind—all the desires or things of the flesh. It is that part of us that *must* surrender to the Spirit of God; that part that *must* be renewed by the Word of God in order to be able to live or walk in the Spirit. Instead of complaining about his problems or burdens, David was awestruck with God's ways, attributes, character as well as His blessings upon his life. He came to the realization of the faithfulness of God to all His creation, and with all these springing up from the depth of his heart came his prayers of praise and adoration to God. David saw God as the self-existing one, who has no end—the almighty.

The Word of God tells us that, in everything (in every circumstance), we should give thanks, as this is the will of God in Christ Jesus (1 Thessalonians 5:18). We must surrender fully to the Lordship of God, allowing Him to be the master of our lives, and making Him the center of our existence. Let us bless the Lord with all our being—body, spirit, and soul, leaving nothing out. God is worthy of our praise because of who He is and all that He has done. David reminded himself of the loving kindness of God: the forgiver of sins, the healer of all our diseases, the redeemer of our lives from the pit, the one who crowns us with love and compassion, who satisfies our desires with good things, and renews our youth like the eagle's (Psalms 103:3–5 NKJV). "For as high as the heavens are above the earth, so great is His love for those who fear Him; as far as the east is from the west, so far has He removed our transgressions from us." (Psalms 103:11–12 NIV). "But from everlasting to everlasting, the LORD'S love is with those who fear Him, and His righteousness with their children's children—with those who keep His covenant and remember to obey His precepts." (Psalms 103:17–18 NIV).

In Isaiah, we see how the angels continuously worship the Lord by calling to one another saying, "...Holy, holy, holy is the LORD Almighty; the whole earth is full of His glory." (Isaiah 6:3 NIV). And at the birth of Christ Jesus, the angels declared, "Glory to God in the highest heaven, and on earth peace to those on whom His favor rests." (Luke 2:14 NIV). The twenty-four elders removed their crowns before the throne of God as they cry out, "You are worthy, our Lord and God, to receive glory and honor and power, for You created all things, and by Your will they were created and have their being." (Revelation 4:11 NIV). Angels are constantly worshipping the Lord God. The heavens—stars, moon, and everything in the firmaments, all declare the Lord's glory. We ought to declare in every circumstance His holy name through His Word in the power of His Holy Spirit because there is power in the spoken Word of God. Love the Lord with your entire being, bless and give Him all the praise, honor, and thanks. Know that it is God who has created us for a purpose, and for His glory and pleasure. He chose us and loved us with an everlasting love; we were not born by chance, but we were wonderfully and intentionally created and destined for God's glory. Let us fully surrender to His lordship and allow Him to perfect His will for our lives; and when we take refuge in His unfailing love, and hunger and thirst for more of Him in us and through us, we shall be filled. Let us continuously feed on God's Word and allow it to take root in us and produce good fruits—for the Word of the Lord endures forever and will *never* fail.

THE REASON OF OUR BEING

Everything God created is for a purpose and to meet a specific need or needs. Take a moment out of your busy schedule today and just reflect on some things around you. You will begin to realize the beauty and perfection of creation, and their specific reasons for which they were created by the Lord. On that same note, you and I were wonderfully and perfectly created by the Lord, to praise and fellowship with Him, and to rule over everything the Lord God created on this earth (Genesis 1:26 NIV). *Without God, there is no true purpose in life; without our source of living, there is no true life or fulfillment. Without Christ Jesus, one can do nothing or be nothing that will endure; we need the direction and hand of the Spirit of God in every step of the way. He is all that we need and the reason of human existence.* Let us ask Him today to come into our hearts and be the Lord of our lives; allowing His Holy Spirit to guard our hearts and minds through His Word. The Lord is the one who teaches us what is best and directs us in the way we should go. He is love and in Him there is no darkness; He is the light of the world, the living bread, the good shepherd who laid down His life for us, the faithful father, the covenant keeper, the way, the truth, and the life—Jesus Christ our Lord, God in the flesh. Whoever comes to Him and calls on His name shall be saved. He said, "Behold, I stand at the door, and knock: if any man hears My voice, and open the door, I will come into him, and will sup with him, and he with Me." (Revelation 3:20 KJV). The Lord is knocking on the door of your heart because He loves you; not because of you but because of who He is. He is longing for a relationship with you; hence, He is after your heart and not your sacrifice or service—a willing heart that will fellowship and walk with Him according to His Word. Let us seek the Lord while we have the time, when all is going well, my dear friends, before it is too late; and please do not turn away by hardening your heart. Let Him have His way in you, because everything (including heaven and earth) is only temporal, and is passing away, but God and His Word will *remain forever.*

THE EARTH IS THE LORD'S

Do you really know the God you worship? You may have read a lot about Him, heard about Him your entire life, but do you really know Him *personally?* Knowing God personally will lead you to understanding Him; a person cannot understand the ways of another person without knowing them first. Likewise, when we know the Lord, we understand His character, nature and ways, which helps us develop reverential fear of Him, leading to obedience of His Word. As a result, we become better in serving the Lord because we are familiar with His attributes and the things which are pleasing to Him. For instance, reading and meditating God's Word, as well as talking about Him, or even using His Word in every situation, are some of the ways we can develop the knowledge of God. Moses asked the Lord, "If You are pleased with me, teach me Your ways so I may know You and continue to find favor with You..." (Exodus 33:13 NIV). If you do not know who God is, or you are not sure of His ways, then ask Him to teach you, so that you can know Him, serve Him better, and find favor with Him. Start by asking the Lord Jesus to come into your heart and make you the man or woman

He created you to be. Study His Word (the Bible) and allow His Holy Spirit to teach you His ways, His mind, and His heart. The God we worship is:

> The God who made the world and everything in it is the Lord of heaven and earth and does not live in temples built by human hands. And He is not served by human hands, as if He needed anything. Rather, He Himself gives everyone life and breath and everything else. (Acts 17:24–25 NIV).

God is always willing and waiting for our relationship; He will never turn away from us when we seek Him with every fiber of our being. It is the desire of our heavenly Father like any loving father, for His children to know, love, and fellowship with Him, and this cannot be achieved without knowing Him personally.

God is the king of glory and He is above *all* things—everything on the face of the earth, everything we aspire to or attain belongs to the Lord God Almighty, the creator of them all. So, why do we chase after, worship, and adore created things rather than the creator? Why do people worry about perishable things of this world that are only but for a while, rather than storing up eternal things of God that will never rot or be destroyed? Seek the Lord God with all your being, the king of all kings and the Lord of all lords in your life. Fear the Lord with all reverence and sincerity because of who He is, for all that He has done, and all that He is still doing. Abide in His Word and allow His Word through the power of the Holy Spirit to come alive in you and through you. God is in control of everything, and He is faithful to all His creation; His Word is full of all His promises for those that love Him and heed to His Word. Even though we live in this world, we (children of God) have been translated through our faith in Christ Jesus from the kingdom and ways of this dark world. We now belong to God's kingdom and hence, follow His plan for living, which is the life of Christ Jesus in us. God is the one that our souls should thirst and long for more than anything in this world—to know Him more and more and have a relationship with Him, through His Word and His Holy Spirit. And all the things that we worry about and chase after in this life shall be given to us according to God's will for us.

God created all things perfectly in His beauty and for His pleasure and glory. Everything comes from the earth and to the earth it will all return at the end. From the dust of the earth, God created human and breathed into his nostrils His breath of life, and the human became a living being—with soul and spirit (Genesis 2:7 NKJV). And when we die, our mortal bodies will return to dust but the spirit which is eternal will head back to God and await judgement. Everything that humans would ever need while on this planet earth, God had provided on the face of the earth. That is how faithful our God is! It all belongs to Him (including you and I)! Therefore, God is our *source of everything*. The earth is full of all that we need to survive and enjoy life; everything our senses can experience comes from the earth. All our physical needs, wants, and aspirations are all embedded in the earth—from the air we breathe, to the sun by day, and the moon and stars by night. Even Christ Jesus, during His time on earth, used the things on the earth (dust, mud, and water) to heal the sick. You see, my dear friends in Christ, our God, our heavenly Father, owns it all! What we need is His Holy Spirit in us and at work in us, to help us understand and enjoy the things that God has freely given us (His children). In other words, we must have a relationship with our creator, the giver of life, and sustainer of all things through the Holy Spirit and the Word.

Follow the way of the Lord, stay on the narrow path of the Lord Jesus to eternal life. Do not follow the ways and images of this world but endeavor to be transformed in all areas of your life by renewing your mind, to that of Christ's, through His Word. *Do not worry about anything, but in everything, pray and commit every* circumstance to the Lord according to the Word of God. Remember, God is our refuge, our source of everything, our deliverer, our tower, our strength, our healer, our sustainer, our peace, our provider, our savior, our judge, the way, the truth, and the life. Christ Jesus is our all and in all! God's loving kindness (mercy, grace, goodness, etc.) is far better than life itself, so let us praise and glorify His Holy name in everything that we say and do. God is looking for men and women that will seek after His face or presence (to know Him), rather than seek after His created things. He wants to abide in His people, so that we can live more abundantly. Remember that God's love endures forever, and His faithfulness is unfailing to every promise He has made towards His creation and children!

May the Lord continue to bless and keep you; may He make His face to shine upon you as He reveals Himself more and more to you each day. May you be soaked in His abundant love, grace, mercy, and favor, as He unfolds His glorious nature and character to you through the power in His spoken Word. And may His glorious fragrance in you emanate to others, through Christ Jesus our Lord and God. Amen!

2

GOD IN THE FLESH—JESUS CHRIST

Who is Jesus Christ? This question might seem a bit vague to many people or may even be seen as more of a cliché. When you hear the name 'Jesus Christ' the first thing that comes to mind is that of Christianity—a faith, religion, a prophet, a savior, a good man, and so on and so forth. Understanding who Jesus is, is a revelation that only the Spirit of God Himself can reveal. When you receive this revelation, your whole perspective of Christ Jesus (who He is, who He was, and who He will be when He comes back) will be enlightened forever. Your search about the meaning of life, faith, religion, and so on, will never be the same. My prayer is that the Holy Spirit of God would reveal the person of Jesus Christ to you even as you read this book. When you have the full revelation of Christ, you realize your identity and potential, since Christ is our blueprint and clear picture of our true image. Once you have the clear revelation of Christ, you will pursue after Him and not after man nor material wealth or social group of this world. May the joy of the Lord that filled my heart when I received this revelation of Christ Jesus, also be yours to the overflowing in Jesus' mighty name. Amen! To God be all the glory now and forever more because in Him dwell all the treasures of wisdom and knowledge.

Before we start delving into the person of Christ Jesus, let me ask you a question; did you know that you are from eternity and now living in time on earth? As a child of God, you are from glory and into glory you shall return when you leave this earth, or this earthly cover known as the body. Since we were created in the image and likeness of God; it is the Lord's desire through the power of the Holy Spirit to reveal to us the person of our Lord Jesus Christ. Wow! When the Holy Spirit gave me this revelation to write on the person of our Lord Jesus, I was a little overwhelmed by the whole concept but then He (the Holy Spirit) started revealing to me deeper than ever before who the Lord Jesus is. I believe the Holy Spirit wants us to understand this mystery about the Godhead in the image of Christ Jesus Himself. God wants us to have full knowledge of who He is; so that, our faith, relationship, and work with Him may be more rooted, inspired, and grounded. One way this happens is through our worship. When we understand who God is and what He has done, our relationship and worship becomes meaningful as we will not be worshipping an unknown God but the living God and creator of all things. *True worship will never happen in the church like it should until we have first seen Christ (have a clear knowledge of Him) and seeing Him would not happen until we first hunger and thirst for Him personally.* When Christ Jesus becomes a reality in our lives through His Word and Spirit, then great signs and wonders will happen in our midst. We understand that hungry and thirsty people are always desperate people, and desperate people as you may agree with me, do get results. Once you have the full wisdom and revelation in the knowledge of Christ Jesus, then you will be fully persuaded that whatever He says in His Word will surely come to pass; and you will also be slave to His Word because of His love in you and yours for Him. I know you are as excited as I am as we embark on this deeper spiritual journey with the Holy Spirit—as He reveals profound insights about Christ Jesus our Lord and God.

The image of Christ Jesus is still a mystery to many believers in the body (the church) or even more so to unbelievers. Before we start, let us make one thing clear that, *in the Godhead, there is one God.* Many tend to think that there are three Gods in the Godhead and this gross error had evolved since the spread of Christianity in Europe namely Rome. It is not that there are three Gods but *one God* operating in *three or many offices or titles* as He pleases—*Father, Son, and Holy Spirit.* The Spirit of God in John the revelator revealed the supreme Deity of Christ Jesus as *one God.* As he mentioned in these expressions:

> Grace and peace to you from Him who is, and who was, and who is to come, and from the seven Spirits before His throne, and from Jesus Christ, who is the faithful witness, the firstborn from the dead, and the ruler over the kings of the earth. To Him who loves us and has freed us from our sins by His blood and has made us to be a kingdom and priests to serve His God and Father—to Him be glory and power forever and ever! Amen. (Revelation 1: 4–6 NIV).

These are titles and descriptions of the *one and same person*—the Lord Jesus Christ. Even the disciples struggled with this concept until the time of the Lord's arrest and crucifixion. Christ Jesus had to reveal once more the revelation of who He is—that He is God. As the disciples were still finding it hard to understand Him, they asked questions about who Christ Jesus was, where He said He was going, and questions about the Father. His response to them was this:

If you really know Me, you will know My Father
as well... Anyone who has seen Me has seen the
Father... Don't you believe that I am in the Father,
and that the Father is in Me? The words I say to
you I do not speak on My own authority. Rather,
it is the Father, living in Me, who is doing His
work. Believe Me when I say that I am in the
Father and the Father is in Me; or at least believe
on the evidence of the works themselves. (John
14:7–11 NIV).

Jesus Christ is the invisible Spirit God in the flesh; the Son
of God in the flesh and known as son of man, having all the
fullness of the Father in Him. Once resurrected and ascended
into heaven, He is no longer the son of man, the great prophet or
teacher; but He is the firstborn who is back to the bosom of the
Father. He is now the resurrected king and Lord, who has won
the battle and taken back the mighty power from the devil. Christ
is above all and over all things, to the praise of His glory. Christ
was revealing the mystery of the Father in the flesh, and to save
those in the flesh, to His disciples; but it was hard for the disciples
to comprehend this truth at the time. *The truth that, the God of the
universe would reach out once again in search of His people but this time
to reconcile them back to Himself; all because of His love for you and me.*
The love of the Father is so amazing and so divine (agape kind
of love)! There is no salvation except through the Son of God,
Jesus Christ our Lord; He is the only mediator between God and
His people, and no one else. Christ is still the head of the church
because He is the church. Hence His leadership over the church
through His Holy Spirit, He will not surrender to any person; and
He will never give or share His glory to or with another person or
thing. God's divine plan that was set even before the foundations
of the earth for humans, including all of creation, still stands.

These last communications between Christ Jesus and His disciples clearly explained and helped their unbelief that He was God Himself in the flesh. He decided to step down (from all His dominion and kingdom) into time that He has created; *the creator became the creation!* But why? you may ask; why would God have to do such an act? The simple answer is *love. God is love and love is God; love is the centerpiece of God!* Out of the abundance of His love for the world, He took on flesh as a Son (His one and only Son). The Father gave Himself in the form of a son—*He gave His best and all!* The old ways of atonement for sins in the Old Testament era (i.e., the yearly sacrifices, burnt offerings, and sin offerings using the blood of animals) were not completely pleasing in the sight of God as it could not take away the sins of humans permanently. It was impossible for the blood of bulls and goats to take away sins, and God was not content with such (Hebrews 10: 1–8 NIV). A pure and holy body had to be prepared to be the perfect sacrifice for sin once and for all—Jesus Christ. God took on human form, born of a virgin and lived among us in order to save us from this evil world and to reconcile us back to Himself, all because of love. Hence, Christ Jesus is the complete representation of the invisible God, the exact likeness of the Father. "For God was pleased to have all His fullness dwell in Him, and through Him to reconcile to Himself all things, whether things on earth or things in heaven, by making peace through His blood, shed on the cross." (Colossians 1:19–20 NIV). This is the revelation Christ was trying to reveal to His apostles during their last conversation before His arrest and crucifixion—that He is in the Father and the Father is in Him (That He is God). The entire Bible talks about Christ, the coming messiah, even before He was born.

> In the beginning was the Word, and the Word was with God, and the Word was God. He was with God in the beginning. Through Him all things were created; without Him nothing was made

that has been made. In Him was life, and that life was the light of all mankind. (John 1:1–4 NIV).

Even the most knowledgeable and religious people of old could not understand this mystery of God. If they had known (realized or believed that Christ was the Messiah), they would not have crucified Him. Christ is the creator and sustainer of all things; for it was in Him, for Him, and through Him that all things were created; and He holds all things together including the universe and all of life. His suffering, death, and resurrection has brought us restoration, joy, and peace in every area of our lives. Our debt, punishment, and battle with sin and the devil— all paid and served in full, and the victory is won.

The Word of God tells us that, Christ came to do the will of God, the Father (John 6:38 NIV). He was on a mission to redeem all humanity from their evil ways, which alienated us from God, making us enemies of God through our minds and evil behavior. God who is eternal and omnipotent has the power to be manifested in different forms as He has always done before. So, He humbled Himself and took on flesh as a Son, lived among us, suffered and died on the cross; He rose again as He promised, for our justification, and ascended back into heaven. Christ Jesus endured the cross and became obedient to death, even death on the cross because of the joy that was set before Him. *Our joy of salvation*—that our joy may be complete as we live more abundantly in Him, both now and into eternity. Christ Jesus is not only our savior but our reigning king over all kings and Lord over all lords; in Him was life and that life was the light of every soul. As God's children, we live and have our entire being in His light. His everlasting and unconditional love for humanity made Christ to lay down His life for us; we love Him because He first loved us even before the foundations of the earth (1 John 4:19 NIV). This love of Christ did not end on the day He ascended into heaven, but it continues by Him sending His Holy Spirit to live in those who believe in Him. The Holy Spirit of God is now in us the moment we accept Christ as Lord over our lives. The Holy Spirit is the one who guides, fills, sustains, convicts, teaches, and comforts the believer; He is our leader and helper each step of the way, and He is always there in us, through us, and with us. He will never leave us nor forsake us. We are still living in the dispensation of the Holy Spirit on earth since the day of Pentecost, and it is impossible to live a successful Christian life without the person of the Holy Spirit. The love of God is still available for you through His salvation and the power of the Holy Spirit. There is no greater privilege than to have the Holy Spirit of God living and working in you and through you. We will go deeper into the person of the Holy Spirit later in the book.

Whether you believe in Christ Jesus or not, it does not change who He is or what He has done, but it matters a great deal to you, my dear friends, because believing in Him and having a relationship with your creator will change your entire life here on earth and into eternity. Your entire existence is based upon your relationship with your creator and Lord. That is what matters at the end when you stand before Him in glory (your relationship with Him). God's grace is so abundant upon you, to still maintain His breath of life in you even at this very moment; without God's breath of life and grace, where would you and I be? Yes, my dear friends, what would become of your many plans and dreams without God's breath of life in your nostrils? You would not be here or alive. Christ's loving kindness keeps every part of your being functioning; everything you have in this life is through God's saving grace and love. His love grants us favor and keeps us from the hand of the evil one; every move we make is because of His loving and righteous hands that sustain us. Our entire existence is because of Him, whether we acknowledge Him or not. Understanding that Christ Jesus is the exact representation of the Father in the flesh (fully God and fully man) will change your worship, your relationship, your love, and your reverence towards Him and others. Christ is all that you need; just keep your eyes on Him and Him alone. May He be the center of your life and existence; let your focus be on Him. In your weakness, His strength is made perfect; in your sickness, He is the great physician and your healer—Christ is your source of life, and in Him you are complete.

Our Lord Jesus is the unfailing and unchanging Word of God; *His name is the Word—trustworthy.* The Word (Christ) has all power in heaven and on earth due to His obedience to the will of God. He is the supernatural Word of God—alive, active, and has the power to separate or divide the soul and the spirit, even more to the point of judging the thoughts and attitudes of the heart. Christ Jesus is every spoken Word of God, certain and dynamic; He is the perfecter of every Word of God as He brings every Word of God into being. He is the very 'Word of God, the living Word of God' full of power, love, mercy, and grace. He declared in John 14:12-13 that, whoever believes in Him will do the works that He has done and do even greater. The same Spirit that was at work in Christ Jesus, and the same that raised Him from the grave, is here, right here on earth, living in you and me from the day we surrendered and accepted Christ as our savior. Our faith in Christ is what makes the difference—His presence in our lives through the Holy Spirit at work in us and through us. Without faith in Christ and in His Word, it is impossible to please God or experience the manifestation of His power and glory. All we must do now is abide in His Word through the faith that He has given us, and declare in His mighty name, to the glory of God our Father. Christ has given us the keys to the kingdom, which is *"binding and loosing"* in His mighty name; that name that is above every other name. We bind the things that are not of God in our lives and set loose the things that are of the will of God for us, in the name of Jesus Christ. This is the Word of the Lord and we must simply obey! Christ has loved us with an everlasting love by laying down His life for our redemption; our love for God compels us to obey His commandments. As He mentioned in the book of John saying, "If you love Me, keep My commands." (John 14:15 NIV). God honors the faith of His obedient children; when we hear His voice, we step out in obedience, because of the love that we have for Him. Our action of faith and obedience is the response to His love. So, stand on God's Word with His faith that moves every mountain you face in the mighty name of Jesus because Christ's love is the greatest sacrifice ever!

CHRIST JESUS—THE GREATEST SACRIFICE

On Memorial Day, in the United States, we honor all our service men and women, and those who have gone before us while serving their nation. We honor them with all sincerity of heart because as the Word of God says, "Greater love has no one than this: to lay down one's life for one's friends." (John 15:13 NIV). The service men and women who have gone, have done the greatest sacrifice by dying for the freedom of their beloved nation, and we thank God for the gift of their lives. But as we honor these men and women of service, we must never forget the *greatest eternal sacrifice that Christ Jesus did on the cross for all humanity—our spiritual and eternal redemption.* Christ's sacrifice was not just for earthly freedom (which is temporal) but an eternal one because there is life after we leave this earthly robe of flesh. *There is eternity, and where each person spends their eternity is very crucial and of most importance.* Yes, there is a resurrection after death, and certainly an eternity in every living soul that the Lord has created. The question is, where will you spend your eternity—Heaven or Hell? *God through Christ Jesus humbled Himself to become flesh and to die not just to take away our sins and freedom from the devil's schemes in this world, but most importantly, He died for our eternity with Him.* God's everlasting love for us was clearly demonstrated when He gave His best, His one, and only Son to come and die for our redemption (John 3:16 NIV). A perfect body God prepared once and for all, to pay the prize, serve the sentence, and finally win the battle between humans and the devil; Christ broke the bondage of sin and its shackles on humanity. Every time we reflect and honor our service men and women, may we also reflect on the greatest of all sacrifices done by our Lord Jesus, and what it means for all humanity that believe in Him. When you are in Christ, you know that death is not the end because Christ is the resurrection and the life, and He is coming very soon for His people—both the living and the dead in Him. Christ is not only the greatest sacrifice of all time but also the greatest gift of all time.

CHRIST JESUS—THE GREATEST GIFT OF ALL TIME

Every year, almost every nation in the world celebrates the birth of our Lord Jesus Christ at Christmas. And as we celebrate the greatest gift of all time, let us also be intentional in seeking, finding, and knowing Him (our Lord Jesus), so that, we may worship and serve Him better. Joy to the world, the Lord has come! Indeed, the birth of our Lord and savior Jesus Christ has brought great joy and deliverance into this world for all people, especially for those that believe in and rely totally on Him. This joy is better than anything you could ever think or imagine. It is often referred to as happiness by many people; but this joy that is from above is far better and enduring than happiness. Happiness is sometimes described as an emotion based on circumstances; when circumstances are good, people feel happy, while at the other end of the spectrum, if things do not happen as anticipated, people feel sad and angry. *Happiness is a temporary state, while joy, however, is not a temporal emotional state, but an attitude of the heart, that comes from the Lord Jesus. Joy is eternal; it is permanent, continual, and not necessarily based on something positive happening.* Happiness can disappear with a change in circumstances since it is a temporary emotional state; but *joy remains.* Joy is greater than our present circumstances, and it brings us peace in the middle of a storm because it is from the Lord, and it is not based on situation at any moment in time. Our joy as believers is based on the joy of the Lord, it is from Him alone; this joy that is from above is an exceptional gift that God deposits in the hearts of believers through the Holy Spirit. This unspeakable love and joy can only be found in Christ Jesus. Material wealth and achievements of this world will *never* give any individual that enduring satisfaction of joy. True joy comes from above; from the Father, who is the giver and sustainer of all good and perfect gifts. And, as we gradually progress from mere happiness to that of real joy in the Lord, let us be partakers of the unspeakable love and joy that is in Jesus Christ. The Bible tells us of this unspeakable love and joy in Luke 2:

> Then the angel said to them, "Do not be afraid, for behold, I bring you good tidings of great joy which will be to all people. For there is born to you this day in the City of David a savior, who is Christ the Lord. And this will be the sign to you: You will find a babe wrapped in swaddling clothes, lying in a manger." And suddenly there was with the angel a multitude of the heavenly host praising God and saying: "Glory to God in the highest, and on earth peace, goodwill toward men!" (Luke 2:10–14 NKJV).

The joy of the Lord is what gives us strength; the things that we do that are pleasing in God's sight give us strength and peace through our faith in Christ. The Lord gives us lasting joy and peace when we abide in Him and in His powerful Word.

Thus, the gift of Christmas has been clearly revealed as an indescribable joy of the Lord and not just happiness over the festivities. This fact was attested to by the song writers: Sir Isaac Watts and George Frederick Handel who composed the timeless

Christmas Carol titled "Joy to the World" in 1719. They wrote and sang, "Joy to the world, the Lord is come! Let earth receive her king; let every heart prepare Him room; and heaven and nature sing!" Joy to the world was one of God's priceless gifts to humanity—at the birth of Jesus Christ. The world has tried imitating this divine joy with external events and materials which only evoke happiness but not true joy. It is my prayer that festive seasons such as Christmas bring out the high-spirited joy of the Lord in your life far beyond the man-made excitement of the lights, foods, carols, parties, shopping, family gatherings, glitz, and glamour of this world. From now on, may the true meaning of the festive seasons be joyous to you and your families as you adore the greatest gift of all time, for those who would receive Him into their hearts—Jesus Christ, who is God's reconciliation plan.

JESUS CHRIST—GOD'S RECONCILIATION PLAN

There is nothing worthier than knowing and serving the Lord of hosts; before whom angels bow, heaven and earth adore; it is an honor to worship Him! What a mighty God we serve, my dear friends! No matter the challenges we face in this life, we know that our Lord and savior Jesus Christ has overcome all of them because He has overcome the world. Christ Jesus is still with us because He lives in us through His Holy Spirit in us and at work in us, for His glory. He is the light to our path and indeed the light of the world; and whosoever believes in Him and walk in His path shall never be in the darkness of this world but will have the light of His life. Christ is our light, and we must shine the light of Christ in us in every area of our lives, so that others may see and know that we are His children. You may wonder why our Lord Jesus made the statement that "I am the light of the world. whoever follows Me will never walk-in darkness but will have the Light of Life." (John 8:12 NIV). He is indeed the light and life of the world because we are living in a dark world, at a time of constant evil in the hearts and minds of people; people with depraved minds filled with all kinds of evil and wickedness. The light and life of Christ in a believer illuminates and changes that individual's former life forever—from death to abundant life, flowing into eternity in Christ. Sin is the failure to attain the standard God has set, a perversion of our nature; it is a breaking of God's holy command for man, and a rebellion against our creator. In other words, sin is simply doing anything that does not glorify God; and when that happens, God removes His presence from us (making us spiritually death). This is because God is holy, and He will not tolerate ungodliness in His people or anything that is not holy. It all started at the beginning of God's creation in the Garden of Eden (Genesis 3); the first man and woman (Adam and Eve) that the Lord God created disobeyed God and sin entered the world; through their disobedience, all of humanity fell short of the glory of God. Humanity became separated from God the Father due to our sinful nature (in our minds and actions), and death came as a result of sin. Hence, all of humanity deserved God's eternal punishment—physical, spiritual and eternal death. *The fleeting pleasure of sin in our lives will never be worth the extreme price we must pay for it, which is God's judgment and eternal damnation.* God blesses obedience but punishes disobedience. Thank God for the precious blood of Christ, that has cleansed us (those that believe in Him) from all unrighteousness!

But God demonstrated His love for us through His one and only Son Jesus Christ who came and died for us; as a ransom to serve our sentence and pay our debt of sin since man could not go to Him because of our sinful nature (John 3:16; Romans 5:8 NIV)—Jesus Christ is God's reconciliation plan. He took the punishment that we all deserved upon Himself. Even though we did not deserve God's love, Christ still reconciled us back to the Father through His obedience to death and His resurrection. The righteous act of our Lord Jesus Christ resulted in our justification and life; through one man's obedience on the cross, the many who receive Him and what He has done are made righteous through faith. The grace of God reigns through righteousness to bring eternal life to those who receive Him. God the Father made Christ Jesus, who had no sin and did not deserve the punishment, to be sin for us, so that in Him we might become the righteousness of God (2 Corinthians 5:21 NIV). This was God's plan to reconcile the world back to Himself in Christ, by not punishing humanity based on their sins. Praise the name of the living God! So, please accept the Lord Jesus and be saved, if you have not come to the saving grace of God, namely Christ Jesus!

Apostle Paul mentioned that, "Therefore, if anyone is in Christ, he is a new creation; old things have passed away; behold, all things have become new." (2 Corinthians 5:17 NKJV). When you become a child of God through faith in Christ, and walk in His Spirit and Word, you become a new creation (born again) in your mind and in your actions. The old you is no more but you have now become a brand-new person in the mind of Christ according to His Word in you. This is the joy that was set before Christ and the reason for which He willingly laid down His life to redeem a sinful world. He is our light and our salvation; His death on the cross paid the price for our sins, if only we will turn to Him with a repentant heart and trust Him as our savior in all areas of our lives. Things may seem to be going well with you but, they are not without the Spirit of God; if your plans are not planted and rooted in the Lord's plan, they will not come to an expected end. Only God's divine plan for our lives prevail to the glory of God the Father. Friends, when you realize the depth of God's love for you, your life will never be the same; when Christ Jesus becomes so tangible to you (who He is and what He has done for you), you will be changed forever from inside out. Allow the Lord Jesus to have His way in you through faith in Him because we have been saved through His mercy and grace.

So, stand on His life changing Word and let it change your life forever because of the power in the spoken Word of God.

THE MERCY AND GRACE OF GOD

Hallelujah! Praise the name of the Lord, who was and is, and is to come! Blessed is He who comes in the name of the Lord! Hosanna in the highest! I get excited in the Spirit whenever I think about God's abundant grace and mercy upon us; and it is an honor to be adopted into the family of God and called children of God, the creator of *all* things. He is a good God, a loving Father, faithful Lord and master; He is just and righteous, whose ways are perfect and true. The Father has loved us with an everlasting love and does not treat us according to our deeds, for His mercy and grace are sufficient for us because of what Christ Jesus did on the cross for us. I am eternally grateful for such a privilege to fellowship or share with you the Word of God through the most awesome gift, power and leadership of the Holy Spirit, who is our teacher, guide, and helper in Christ Jesus. To Him be all glory, honor, and power forever and ever! Amen.

As children of God, we have come to understand that God is a merciful God, and that is one of His characters as a loving Father. But what is the *mercy of God,* as one may ask? *God's mercy is simply, God not treating or punishing us as our sins deserve.* The mercy of God is one of the key foundations of our salvation—derived from the original sin of Adam and Eve in the Garden of Eden. The Word tells us that, we have all sinned and fallen short of the glory of God and deserve the full punishment of God, which is death (Romans 3:23 NKJV). And "The wages of sin is death, but the gift of God is eternal life in Christ Jesus our Lord." (Romans 6:23 NIV). God put our punishment on Christ Jesus through His sacrificial death on the cross for us, and when we accept His sacrifice through our faith in Him, we become children of God—no more under the law of sin and death, no more slaves to sin, or bound by our sinful desires but now slaves to righteousness through our faith in Christ Jesus. Hallelujah!! God's mercy is sufficient to overcome any mountain in your life; He is always ready to overshadow you with His love and mercy because it is not His will that any person should perish. For God so loved the world (you and me) that He gave Himself as a Son through Jesus Christ (to die for us), that whosoever believes in Him (in what He has done on the cross) shall not perish (shall not be condemned to eternal damnation) but have everlasting life in Christ Jesus (John 3:16 NIV). God's love for us is clearly demonstrated in His mercy upon us; His mercy is continual, and it is for anyone who accepts it now and forever. The Bible tells us that, "If by the trespass of one man, death reigned through that one man, how much more will those who receive God's abundant provision of grace and of the gift of righteousness reign in life through the one man, Jesus Christ!" (Romans 5:17 NIV). Hence, through the obedience of Christ Jesus to the will of the Father, many who believe are made righteous through His saving grace.

The grace of God again is, God blessing us with His loving-kindness regardless of our sins; God loving or treating us with kindness when we do not deserve or merit it at all. In other words, God choosing to love us regardless of our past, present, or future wrongs. Regardless of who we are, through our faith in Christ Jesus, we all share in this amazing grace of God. *God see us all as one in Christ (one people and one body in Him); He does not see or take into consideration our color, status, birthplace, achievements, ability, disability, or knowledge; God only sees a heart after His heart because that is all that matters.* Through Christ Jesus, we are now under the saving grace of God, and His grace is sufficient and able to forgive and overcome any sin. Nevertheless, my friends, as a new creation in Christ, we cannot continue to live in our sinful nature or in our old ways because we have the grace of God available for us. We must endeavor to be slaves to righteousness as we put away the old deeds that are enmity to God through the help of the

Holy Spirit in us. We must intentionally continue to renew our minds with the Word of God and fellowship in prayer. As apostle Paul mentioned in the book of Ephesians, "But because of His great love for us, God who is rich in mercy, made us alive with our Lord Jesus even when we were dead in transgressions—it is by grace you have been saved." (Ephesians 2:4–5 NIV). We have been saved only by God's incomparable riches of grace or His unmerited grace through our faith in Christ Jesus; and it is never by our efforts, ideologies, deeds, or hard works.

God's grace upon us through faith in Christ Jesus has not only given us abundant life here on earth but also eternal life in Him. We are now translated from death into everlasting life with Christ, without going through judgement, on judgement day. Our names are now written in the Lambs Book of Life because of our faith in Christ Jesus, in His Word, and in His Holy Spirit. God has also given us boldness through the Holy Spirit in our work with Him; supernatural confidence that only comes through faith and through the Spirit of God. We can now come freely with confidence to God's presence as His children (born of His Spirit and mind), for His mercy, grace, and direction to help us in time of our needs. Through God's grace, we develop strength and grow in the knowledge and revelation of Him, which is vital in our relationship with the Lord. Through His grace, we are also able to understand our identity (who we are in Christ), knowing for sure that we have been redeemed, justified, and set apart with an inheritance in the Lord for greater work, to the glory of God our Father. Our lifestyle must reflect that of our image (Christ) through His saving grace that is so abundant upon us that believe in His salvation. May you continue to abide in God's great mercy and grace through your fruits—in your daily lifestyle and relationship with others. May the fragrance of God's love and light in you through Christ, spread to all around you, to the glory of God our Father. And may His peace that exceeds all human knowledge and understanding guide your heart and mind, through Christ Jesus our Lord. Amen!

JESUS THE BREAD OF LIFE

Christ Jesus is the *bread of life*—He is the giver and sustainer of life itself; and we must feed on Him to live abundantly. When you feed on the Word of God and from His Holy Spirit friends, you are bound to live life abundantly in the joy and peace that only comes from the Lord; you will live, because He lives, no matter what the enemy throws at you. You will overcome because the Lord has already overcome the devil on the cross. It is indeed finished! Christ is seated in heaven interceding on our behalf and His Holy Spirit is here on earth with us helping us that believe in Him. God's holy plan of reconciliation of humanity stands forever. The Jewish people during the time of Christ Jesus could not accept the Lord as the messiah of the world even though the entire Old Testament or Jewish Torah prophesied about the events of the coming messiah. You may wonder, and I still cannot fathom how they could have missed such an event; but yes, they did miss it and so the Scripture was fulfilled. Christ's own people did not receive Him—the people He had formed with His own hands, the only people He had saved from the land of slavery as His own and had performed miraculous signs and wonders on their behalf; these same people could not accept Him, they rejected Him. Thus, to us that receive Him (Christ Jesus) He has given the power to become children of God, even to us that believe in His name (John 1:11–13 NIV). As we mentioned earlier, even the disciples struggled with their faith in our Lord Jesus; so, Christ kept revealing His identity to them in the gospel of John, using the phrase "*I am.*" To name a few, "I am the bread of life, I am the light of the world, I am the door, I am the good shepherd, I am the resurrection and the life, I am the way, the truth and the life, I am the vine, I am the alpha and the omega, the first and the last, the beginning and the end." (John 6:35; John 8:12; John 10:7–11; John 11:25–26; John 14:6; John 15:5; Revelation 22:13 NIV). Christ was clearly revealing to them that He is the same God of the Israelites—the infinite one, the eternal God, sovereign one, all powerful, unchanging in character and nature, the creator, and almighty God.

In John's gospel, Jesus declared, "I am the bread of life. Whoever comes to Me will never go hungry, and whoever believes in Me will never be thirsty." (John 6:35 NIV). In this passage, we see that Christ was having a long conversation with some of the 5000 people He had just finished feeding using five loaves and two fishes. The crowd continued to follow Him after that miracle, not because of the miraculous signs performed but because they ate the loaves and were filled, as Jesus informed them. He continued the communication by saying to them, "Do not work for food that spoils, but for food that endures to eternal life, which the son of man will give you. For on Him God the Father has placed His seal of approval. Why spend money on what is not bread and labor on what does not satisfy? Listen, listen to Me, and eat what is Good… listen that you may live." (John 6:27 NIV). Christ Jesus is the living bread of God that comes from heaven to give life to the world; to those that believe in Him. When you feed on the Word of God, feed from the Lord Jesus and His Holy Spirit, you will surely be satisfied as He is the life-giving bread that fills the empty vacuum of the human soul. That void in the human soul that nothing in this world can satisfy but the Spirit of the living God; only Christ is the true manna (bread) from heaven.

Jesus is the living manna that came down from heaven with the seal of approval from the Father to do His will of salvation; and whoever feeds on Him will never go hungry or thirsty as they will live forever. Unless one believes in Christ Jesus and be saved, such a person will continue to chase after perishable or temporary things of this world with no true satisfaction. Nothing in this world (no amount of wealth, fame, achievements, material things, or knowledge) can satisfy the human soul, except the living bread of God that came down from the Father—Jesus Christ. The Lord Jesus continues saying, "Just as the living Father sent Me and I live because of the Father, so the one who feeds on Me will live because of Me." (John 6: 57 NIV). If you feed on Christ Jesus, you will live forever because His Holy Spirit in you gives life and life eternal, and the flesh accounts for nothing. Remember, every spoken Word of God is Spirit and life because God is a Spirit and you and I were formed in His image and likeness. Hence, we must reflect the image and character of God in all totality through the help of His Holy Spirit who reside in us the moment we accept the Lord Jesus as our savior. *As you feed your physical body in order to live; likewise, you must feed your spirit in order to grow spiritually.* Let us feed on Christ Jesus, feed on His Word, His life, His mindset, His character, and His ways. There is nothing like 'my life, and my way,' there is only one way and one life—the way of the Lord Jesus. He said, "I am the way and the truth and the life. No one comes to the Father except through Me." (John 14:6 NIV). Christ is our example in order to live life more abundantly in this world and forevermore.

If you do not have a relationship with your creator, now is the time to start one; tomorrow might be too late. Seek the Lord Jesus now while you have the chance, while He may be found; call on Him while He is near you, forsake your ways, and surrender to His ways today. "Surely the arm of the Lord is not too short to save, nor His ears too dull to hear. But your iniquities have separated you from your God; your sins have hidden His face from you, so that He will not hear." (Isaiah 59:1–2 NIV). *There is no one so down and out or no situation that is beyond God's love and saving grace.* When you return to God with a penitent heart, He will never reject you because it is not the Father's will for anyone to perish. Hence, it is no coincidence or by chance that you are reading this book; it is a divine appointment—an appointment made by the Lord God Himself. To Him be all the glory now and forever! Amen! Christ came to this dying world to bring life and restoration through His obedience on the cross for you and me; He came to give us spiritual food and to restore our lives back to the Father—to bind up the wounds of this life, heal the broken hearted, give freedom to those bound by the enemy, set the captives free, open the eyes of those who are blind to the things of God, to comfort, and give joy and peace. Christ willingly laid down His life to give us ours; so, feed on Him because He is the true living bread of life. May the Lord Jesus Christ clothe you with the garment of salvation and cover you with His robe of righteousness; may you realize the depth of God's love for you through Jesus Christ our Lord. May you be filled more than ever before with the knowledge and revelation of the Lord Jesus, through the power of His Word. And may you have a personal encounter with Him that will change you forever, into the man or woman, He intended you to be. Amen!

Christ continued to reveal His identity to His disciples saying, "I am the light of the world. He who follows Me shall not walk in darkness but have the light of life." (John 8:12 NKJV). He made this profound statement as He was in the temple during the feast of the tabernacles where He rescued the woman about to be stoned for adultery, and then proclaimed to those who watched the event. In this verse, the Lord Jesus is exclusively declaring Himself to be the light of the world and that He is the source of spiritual light to the world. He speaks of the light of His truth, the light of His Word, the light of eternal life, the light of His Spirit; those who perceive the true light will never walk in spiritual darkness. He is the light of the world, and if you have Him as your Lord and savior, He will light your path, guide and protect you in your life's journey through the fellowship with His Spirit in you. As we continue our spiritual walk with the Lord, the light of Jesus Christ in us must be taken and applied into the darkness of sin that swamps the hearts of unbelievers or those who are not following

Him. The reverse is also true, if we fail to walk with the Lord or follow Him, we will not have the light of life, and our world will be full of darkness and bondage.

Let us pay close attention to the wellbeing of our spiritual lives; for our spiritual lives to function according to God's perfect will, we must have His spiritual light that comes only from Him—our Lord Jesus Christ. The Bible tells us that no man can come into the spiritual light of Jesus Christ, unless God enables him or her. God's light in us compels us to focus on spiritual things such as fellowship, prayer, love, His Word, seeking His face, and knowing Him. These things do not always happen in the absence of God's light. You can see that this is not the case for unbelievers, as unbelievers do not welcome this light because the light exposes their dark world, and they hate the light. Our Lord Jesus promised us that when we follow Him, we will never work in darkness; we will never follow the ways of sin or live in a state of continually sinning; we repent of our sins to stay close to the light of the world. The other promise is that when we follow Christ, we will reflect the light of life. And just as He came as the light of the world, He also commands us to be lights, too (Matthew 5:14–16 NIV).

Daniel also talked about this light as he praised the sovereign God for revealing king Nebuchadnezzar's dream to him by saying:

> Blessed be the name of God forever and ever, for wisdom and might are His. And He changes the times and the seasons; He removes kings and raises up kings; He gives wisdom to the wise and knowledge to those who have understanding. He reveals deep and secret things; He knows what is in the darkness, and light dwells with Him." (Daniel 2:20–23 NKJV).

You see, 'darkness', in a spiritual sense, mostly refers to sin or confusion about the truth, namely, Christ Jesus. *Just as in life, the darkness can coat evil or misrepresent what is real; likewise, in the spiritual world, it can misrepresent the truth and makes it difficult to see or know the truth.* Christ Jesus wants us to live out our lives in the light, and that light comes from Him.

Our Lord Jesus Christ came to earth to fulfill the will of God and fulfill the prophecies about the promised messiah and Lord. He promised to come and redeem us from our sins, and in summary of His short ministry here on earth, Christ healed the sick and raised the dead. Full of respect, He treated others with respect including those who were treated by the world as nothing. Christ gave up everything and devoted His life to proclaiming the good news of the gospel. At the end of His time on earth, He took on Himself the sins of the world and then willingly allowed Himself to be crucified. He conquered death and rose again to reconcile us to Himself. Christ Jesus is indeed the light of the world, even though He is not with us physically (in bodily form) on earth, but He is with us in the form of His Holy Spirit in us (in those that believe in Him and live by His Word and Holy Spirit). We can still be guided by His light if we chose to follow Him. The light of Christ, which is the light of life, is available to any one of us if we choose to follow Him. Hence, darkness of the enemy shall never prevail in us when we dwell in God's presence of light.

DARKNESS SHALL NEVER PREVAIL IN THE PRESENCE OF LIGHT

Jesus is the light of the world—the source of spiritual light to this dark world! He promised us that when we follow Him, we will never walk in darkness; we will never follow the ways of sin or live in a state of continually sinning. When we follow Christ, we repent of our sins to stay close to the light of the world. That light is Christ Jesus in you, so walk in the light and let it shine for His glory. Let the light of Christ shines through your actions, words, and through your thoughts according to His will. Thus, the power of darkness shall never overpower you because the Spirit of His light is in you. According to the gospel of John, "The light shines in the darkness, and the darkness has not overcome it." (John 1:5 NIV). Light always shines in the darkness and the darkness shall never prevail in the presence of light; God is light, and in His presence, no darkness will prevail or stand. When the light of Christ is in you, you will abide in Him and His Word will abide in you; darkness will have no power over you. When Christ Jesus is in you, no shadow of darkness, no shadow of unbelief, no shadow of temptation, no shadow of hate, no shadow of powerlessness, or hopelessness shall overpower you. When the light is in you, you become slave to righteousness, and not slave to sin or darkness anymore. When the light is in you, the fruit of the Spirit of God will show forth as evidence of His presence in you. My dear friends in Christ, let us be encouraged by the prophet Isaiah saying, "Arise, shine, for your light has come, and the glory of the Lord has risen upon you!" (Isaiah 60:1 NIV). Indeed, our light has come, and the glory of the Father has been revealed in the face of Christ Jesus, our Lord. Hence forth, let us act and live like people of light in this dark world, and let every aspect of our lives reflect the light of Christ in us through the power of His Word. Amen! Christ Jesus is our peace through the justification of our faith in Him.

CHRIST IS OUR PEACE

Christ Jesus has made us one people in Him, and He is now our peace! *In Christ we are: one people, one body, united, working together, one family, one nation, indivisible, joined together, connected, and one spirit.* The power of the cross has destroyed the pull factors that have separated God's people. The Amplified Bible puts it this way:

For He is [Himself] our peace (our bond of unity and harmony). He has made us both [Jew and Gentile] one [body], and has broken down (destroyed, abolished) the hostile dividing wall between us, by abolishing in His [own crucified] flesh the enmity [caused by] the Law with its decrees and ordinances [which He annulled]; that He from the two might create in Himself one new man, [one new quality of humanity out of the two], so making peace. (Ephesians 2:14–15 AMPC).

Christ reconciled to God both Jew and Gentile, circumcised, and uncircumcised, united in a single body by means of His cross, thereby killing the mutual enmity and bringing the feud to an end. Christ Jesus came and preached the glad tidings of peace to you and me who were afar (Gentiles) and to those who were nearby (Jews). For it is through Him that we both now have an introduction or access by one Holy Spirit to the Father so that we can approach God. Therefore, we are no longer outsiders (exiles, migrants, and aliens, excluded from the rights of citizens), but we now share citizenship with the saints (God's own people, consecrated, and set apart, for Himself)—we belong to God's own household through the precious blood of Christ. We are built upon the foundation of the apostles and prophets with Christ Jesus Himself the chief cornerstone. In Him the whole structure is joined together harmoniously, and it continues to rise or grow into a holy temple in the Lord. In Christ, and in fellowship with one another you yourselves also are being built up into this structure with the rest, to form a fixed abode or dwelling place of God through His Spirit. (Ephesians 2:14–22 AMPC).

The message is simple, Christ Jesus has broken down the middle "wall of partition" or "dividing wall of hostility" that divided Jews and Gentiles (believer and non-believers), and He has made the two one new people (Ephesians 2:14 KJV). The veil of division has been torn apart at the event on the cross; we can all go boldly into the presence of God now and seek help in time of trouble through our faith in Christ Jesus. In this context, the apostle Paul was addressing Christians of both Jewish and Gentile backgrounds, where there had been a socially dividing wall that had segregated them. Paul was speaking of the division among God's people. The same is true today in this generation of ours; we have allowed the devil, Satan, the deceiver, and the evil one to tear us apart socially, culturally, economically, physically, spiritually, nationally, and internationally. These dividing walls are everywhere my friends. The church had also experienced similar divisions according to Acts 15:5 and Galatians 2:11. Even our Lord Jesus made mention of a wall around a vineyard in Matthew 21:33 and Mark 12:1. However, in Christ, this division or hostility was broken down. Hallelujah! *Now, there is no distinction between Jews and Gentiles in Christ Jesus—in Christ Jesus we are all one body. In Him there is no male or female, no bond or free, no black or white, no rich or poor. In Christ, we are one family through the power of the cross of Christ Jesus our Lord.* Christ's love for us is more than anything! The Word of God tells us in Ephesians:

> [That you may really come] to know [practically, through experience for yourselves] the love of Christ, which far surpasses mere knowledge [without experience]; that you may be filled [through all your being] unto all the fullness of God [may have the richest measure of the divine Presence, and become a body wholly filled and flooded with God Himself]! Now to Him Who, by (in consequence of) the [action of His] power that is at work within us, is able to [carry out His purpose and] do superabundantly, far over and above all that we [dare] ask or think

[infinitely beyond our highest prayers, desires, thoughts, hopes, or dreams]—To Him be glory in the church and in Christ Jesus throughout all generations forever and ever. Amen (so be it). (Ephesians 3: 19–21 AMPC).

Christ is the only one that can give us peace; without Him there can never be *true peace* in this world. Through the power of the cross, Christ has reconciled us back to God, and made us one people and given us His peace that surpasses all human knowledge and understanding through the presence of His Holy Spirit in us that believe in Him. Through faith in Christ, we are now children of God; we are all the same through the eyes of faith. As believers in the Lord Jesus, we are all one body, one people, one nation, and we walk in one Holy Spirit! Amen. God sees His children through the blood of Jesus Christ our Lord and His mercy and love. In Christ, there is only *'one race,'* which is the *'human race'* (God's people, one people in Christ). Christ Jesus is our hope through His life and resurrection from the grave; let us abide and live in this hope.

CHRIST'S RESURRECTION—OUR HOPE

The Word of God tells us that Christ Jesus died for the sins of the world (past, present and future); He became the atoning sacrifice on the cross for our sins (to pay in full the debt, sentence, and judgement that you and I deserve for our sins). The Lord Jesus has simply won the battle against sin, the devil, and his devices of pain, sickness, disease, death, and hopelessness. However, Christ did not stay on the cross or in the grave, He rose again on the third day, and later ascended into heaven for our justification. If Christ had not risen or resurrected, Christianity would have been in vain. Therefore, there is supernatural power in His resurrection; there is eternal victory because of His resurrection. The resurrection is our hope as Christians, and as believers in the Lord Jesus Christ. The apostles were energized when the Holy Spirit came upon them on the day of Pentecost after the resurrection and ascension of Christ. The same Holy Spirit that raised our Lord Jesus from the dead filled the apostles, and they began to speak in different languages as the Holy Spirit lead them and gave then utterance (Acts 2:1–4 NIV). The apostles, as a result, were filled with *boldness and power* of the Holy Spirit; the same people that denied Christ and ran away from Him, were now on fire to declare the good news of the gospel. Apostle Peter who had denied the Lord three times was now filled with the Holy Spirit and boldly addressed the confused crowd saying:

> Men of Israel, hear these words: Jesus of Nazareth, a Man attested by God to you by miracles, wonders, and signs which God did through Him in your midst, as you yourselves also know— Him, being delivered by the determined counsel and foreknowledge of God, you have taken by lawless hands, have crucified and put to death; whom God raised up, having loosed the pains of death, because it was not possible that He should be held by it. (Act 2:22–24 NKJV).

In addition, Peter then warned the assembled multitude saying, "Repent and let every one of you be baptized in the name of Jesus Christ for the remission of sins; and you shall receive the gift of the Holy Spirit." (Act 2:38 NKJV). He spoke with such power and conviction that his listeners were *cut to the heart* (with remorse and anxiety). (verse 37). That very day, 3,000 individuals determined to follow and surrender their lives to the Lord Jesus' way of life, and they were baptized. My dear friends, be determined to follow Jesus Christ! When a seed is planted, it dies before coming alive to produce many. Likewise, Christ had to die (He freely laid down His life) in order to come alive forever and produce much fruit in us (so that we may live abundantly in this life and into eternity). Therefore, when you die to yourself and accept what has been done for your sins on the cross, you become alive in Him and His Holy Spirit becomes your leader in all areas of your life. You see the resurrection as your hope and strength—your hope of abundant life, your hope of eternal life, your hope for the future, your assurance, and your freedom from Satan's bondage of darkness including sin and death.

The resurrection power of the Lord Jesus continues to work in us until the day He comes. The victory of that glorious Pentecostal morning is forever at work in us and through us as children of God through faith in Christ Jesus. Apostle Paul mentioned once more in Romans, "And if the Spirit of Him who raised Jesus from the dead lives in you, He who raised Christ Jesus from the dead will also give life to your mortal bodies through His Spirit, who lives in you." (Romans 8:11 AMP). And yes, that same Holy Spirit is living in us, that believe in the Lord Jesus; teaching, guiding, and leading us into parts of righteousness for His name's sake. However, many Christians of today live without the leadership of the Holy Spirit in their lives; they talk about Him but deny His power and role even in the church. *But there is no true Christianity without the leadership of the Holy Spirit because Christianity was birthed upon the leadership of the Holy Spirit. He is the rock upon which Christianity was built, and this has not changed; God's plan and Word still stands.* Christ mentioned the Holy Spirit during His final comforting discourse with His disciples in the gospel of John, "And I will ask the Father, and He will give you another advocate to help you and be with you—the Spirit of truth. The world cannot accept Him because it neither sees Him nor knows Him. But you know Him, for He lives with you and will be in you." (John, 14:17 NIV). When you accept the Lord Jesus as your personal savior, His Holy Spirit comes and takes His place in your heart as a child of God—reminding you of God's Word, renewing your mind with His Word, teaching you, guiding you in all areas of your life, advocating on your behalf, and leading you in all things concerning the kingdom of God. Since God is a Spirit, it only takes the Spirit of God to reveal the mind of God through His Word; only the Holy Spirit can give us the revelation and knowledge of the kingdom and things of God. Without the presence of the Holy Spirit in an individual, he or she can *never* understand the mystery of God's kingdom, His character, nature, and what He has freely given us as His children. It is the Holy Spirit that reveals the deep things of God to His children; this is the Spirit that we have received, and it is not the spirit of the world but the Spirit from God Himself. We will go deeper into the person of the Holy Spirit later in the book.

As stated before, Christ Jesus' resurrection gives us hope and an assurance for the future because He has overcome the world, sin, death, and the grave. We are now more than conquerors through Christ Jesus; and whatever we ask the Father in His name (the name of Jesus Christ) shall be done according to the will of God. And because of our faith in Him, we will do even greater things, since Christ is now seated in heaven at the right hand of the Father (John 14:12–14 NIV). The Lord is now exalted far above all rule, authority, powers, principalities, and dominion. His name is above all other names, and at the mention of His name, everything (if it has a name) *must bow*—things in heaven, on earth, and under the earth. *This is our victory in Christ, and we must walk in this victory and power of our resurrected king; we must know who and whose we are in Christ, and at what price we have been bought. Even though we live in this world, yet we are no more of this world but of the kingdom of God, and in the kingdom of God, all things are possible in Christ.*

The resurrection is our freedom from Satan's bondage of sin, death, and the grave. On the cross, Christ cried out, "It is finished!" (John 19:30 NIV). Meaning that, it is *paid for in full*— our sins, guilt, sickness, pain, disappointments, sufferings, fear, and so on and so forth. Sin has no hold on you anymore because the Spirit of God now lives in you guiding and leading you. The fear of death and the grave has been conquered forever at the cross and in the resurrection. We now have abundant and eternal life in Christ Jesus because we believe and trust in Him. Praise the name of the living God, for great things He has done! The Lord is our hope and answer for today and the future; His resurrection is indeed our confidence in this dark world, and we must keep our eyes on this victory, which is in Christ Jesus. Let us walk daily in this victory my dear friends, let it be our lifestyle as we declare the unchanging Word of God. The Lord Jesus is the *only* answer for today, the answer for this time and generation; call on Him!

JESUS IS THE ANSWER FOR TODAY

The prophet Daniel states that, "Those who do wickedly against the covenant He shall corrupt with flattery but the people who know their God shall be strong and carry out great exploits." (Daniel 11:32 NKJV). Do you understand who God truly is or do you have the true knowledge about the Father? As stated earlier, *when you understand who God is, His sovereignty, and what He has done, you will know how to interact with Him, enjoy an eternal relationship with Him, and live an abundant life in Him.* Knowing whom we have believed and serve makes all the difference my dear friends in the Lord. When you know something or someone, it shows that you have an understanding or knowledge of that someone or something; it is a state of being aware of something or someone. Also, when you understand, you can comprehend; you have insight or good judgement—knowing is a matter of the heart. Do you have a heart for the Lord as king David did? King David sought after the heart of God, to please God in every way possible; He loved the Lord God; does that mean that He was a perfect man without sin? Not at all, but He had a heart for the Lord because the Spirit of the Lord was upon Him and guided him into paths of righteousness. When you know and understand the authority that you operate under, you will act in such full assurance and confidence. When the eyes of your understanding (the heart) have been enlightened by the power of the Holy Spirit, you will realize the hope to which the Lord Jesus has called you (eternal life), the depth of His love for you, and your inheritance in Him. Know that we have been bought at a high price, which is the precious blood and life of Christ Jesus, shed for us! Take for instance, the police officers' understanding of authority; every police officer knows the authority he or she operates under, and hence, gives order with confidence. Equally, when you truly know and understand the Lord God through Christ, and He knows you, and His Word abides in you, your life will never be the same again. No matter what goes on around you, you will be at peace knowing for sure that, God is still in control of all His creation, and you are certain that heaven rules! The Holy Spirit reassures us that it does not matter the present situation in our societies or world, God is still Lord over all; He has the final say concerning our lives. The earth is still God's and all its fullness thereof, (everything belongs to the creator) and Christ is forever Lord of all.

The Bible reminds us that Christ Jesus is the creator of all things, the giver of life, the sustainer of all things, the restorer and keeper of our souls, the healer, the provider, the comforter, the advocate, the truth, the way to the Father, the savior, the good shepherd, the life, and our all and in all. When you totally surrender to His leadership, He will certainly take care of you; He promised that He will never leave you or forsake you (Deuteronomy 31:6 NIV). *The problem is not your neighbor, nor your family, your colleagues at work, your race, your socioeconomic status, your language, your politicians, or leaders; the problem is the fact that people need the Lord!* When you have the Lord Jesus in your life, it changes everything about you and around you because you will reflect the love and light of Christ to those around you. As humans, we have all sinned in one way or another, and are far from been perfect; we are not fit to stand in God's presence as we have fallen short of the glory of God through our sinful minds and ways. We as a people of God and as a nation, have turned away from the Lord our God; we have gone after other gods or idols in place of the Lord God almighty, who had established us as His people and nation. As a result of our rebellious and adulterous lives, the Lord's face or presence is turned away from us. Nevertheless, God's hands are still stretched out waiting for the return of His prodigal sons and daughters. His plea is still the same, "If My people who are called by My name, will humble themselves and pray and seek My face and turn from their wicked ways, then I will hear from heaven, and I will forgive their sins and will heal their land." (2 Chronicles 7:14 NIV). We need to return to the Lord almighty and He will forgive us and heal our land; we need a revival in the hearts and spirits of people, a hunger and thirst for the living God. We need an awakening in our churches, in our homes, in our communities, and in our world. We need the fear of God to surpass the fear of people. We must go back into the Word of God and allow His Holy Spirit who is the Spirit of all wisdom and revelation to give us understanding and knowledge of our Father God. We must know whom we have believed and be fully persuaded that He is able to keep every promise He has made concerning His children. Then the love of God will overshadow us as the waters cover the sea, and we will begin to walk in divine health, prosperity, faith, favor, love, and revelation of God. We will begin to live in the mind and character of Christ Jesus, with compassion, love, and kindness towards one another. Christ Jesus is indeed the answer for today; the answer is not found in any other place nor in a particular individual. We must follow Christ Jesus' leadership because He is the *only* true and lasting way; all other ways are sinking sand and end in destruction. Christ is our good shepherd, who laid down His life for His sheep (those that believe in Him), so that we could have life more abundantly through our faith in

Him. We belong to His flock, and no one or thing will be able to snatch us away from Him. The thief (the enemy) comes only to steal and kill and destroy; but Christ Jesus came that we may have life and have it more abundantly (John 10:10 NIV). This is always the devil's aim: to steal, kill, and destroy God's plan for our lives; but keep your eyes on the Lord Jesus and on Him alone, not forgetting that His kingdom (the Holy Spirit) is now with us, living within us, and making us more like Him. Do not let your heart to be troubled or anxious because of what is going on in our world or around us, rather continue to seek after the Lord Jesus Christ and His righteousness that comes through faith in Him. Remember that the Lord has already overcome the world and is now seated and in control of everything. May you be edified in the understanding of this revelation, and may you abide in the power and might of the Holy Spirit in Jesus' precious name. Amen! Fear not, for the Lord your God is with you and only He can satisfy and sustain you.

ONLY JESUS CAN SATISFY YOU

Whatever you need in this life is found in Christ Jesus; your satisfaction comes only from the Lord God. In fact, the Word of God tells us that we can do nothing without Him (Christ); our entire existence and sustenance (physical and spiritual) is only found in Christ (John 15:5 NIV). Therefore, we must long after the face and heart of the Father; we must seek after the kingdom of God—making the Lord God, the number one priority in every area of our lives and in everything that we do. The importance of seeking the kingdom of God should not be taken lightly; it should always be placed at the *top* of every list of goals, wants, or aspirations that we could ever put together. God knows our wants are endless, so He has given us the key to finding everlasting satisfaction in His kingdom, which is to seek first the kingdom of

God and His righteousness, then every other thing, every other want, or desire shall be added to us (Matthew 6:33 NIV).

We may acquire all the wealth available in this world, but still never be satisfied; we may have the best jobs, best homes, cars, children, status, and so on and so forth, yet still not be fulfilled within. The more we achieve our human goals, the more we want, and this vicious circle of insatiable human wants will always prevail in our lives if we fail to abide by the Spirit of God in us. If the Spirit of God is in you, and at work in you, you will not live according to the sinful nature of the flesh. The Holy Spirit in you will have your mind set on what the Spirit desires, which are the things of the kingdom of God, those things that will bring glory to the Father. After which, all other things—you name them—shall be given to you from the Father. This is the order that the Lord God has instituted in place long ago, and it stands even now and forever. Matthew, in his gospel tells us that, "Blessed are those who hunger and thirst for righteousness, for they will be filled." (Matthew 5:6 NIV). Merriam Webster defines 'righteousness' as acting in accordance with divine or moral law, justice, free from guilt or sin. In the broadest sense, righteousness can be defined as having a right standing with God, which can only come from God even as He enables us through His Word and Spirit. *It is God that sets the standards of righteousness; God's standard is what defines true righteousness; no amount of man-made effort will result in righteousness. Righteousness comes from above and to be righteous is to be right with God through faith in Christ Jesus our Lord.* It is no more of our works but through our total surrender to the Lord through His Word and Holy Spirit. Only the Lord God can satisfy our longing and hungry souls (Psalms 107:9 NIV). When we have faith in our Lord Jesus, we become righteous through our faith; and His Holy Spirit gives us peace and joy in this impulsive and tumultuous world.

Without Christ, life is unpredictable in our world, and these times are very chaotic. We see people moving up and down, chasing after their insatiable desires. But as we mentioned earlier, everyone is longing for something which can never be found in any other place other than in Christ Jesus. The more we achieve worldly stuff, the more we want more. We can never be satisfied without Christ; He alone can satisfy our desires. We are all God's people wonderfully and perfectly created in His image and likeness for His glory and pleasure. Christ is the good shepherd who loves, protects, guides, provides, comforts, seeks when lost, and even laid down His own life for His beloved sheep (us). We have the understanding that without the good shepherd, the sheep will go astray and even perish. Likewise, without the Lord Jesus in your life, you become helpless, and harassed by the pull factors of this world caused by the devil's schemes. When you accept Christ Jesus as your shepherd, He will lead your every step and you will discover true joy, fulfillment, and peace, that only comes from Christ, and not from any earthly gains and successes. Today, surrender it all at the feet of Christ because He is the chief shepherd, and He loves you with an eternal love; only He alone can satisfy your soul. Stand my dear friends, on the assurance of Christ Jesus and see the salvation of the Lord in your lives; you will experience the loving heart of the Father through His unchanging and powerful Word.

JESUS OUR STRONG TOWER

If you are anxious, worried, heavy laden, and overburdened in your heart and mind, then come! Come and surrender at the feet of the Lord Jesus Christ, at the feet of His mercy and grace. He will ease, renew, restore, and refresh your soul through the power of His Word. The Lord will give you rest and peace because He is the strong tower through faith in Him. Christ Jesus is your shelter in a time of storm; when the waves of this life are roaring like a lion, the Lord is always there to calm your raging sea. He is the rock of our salvation, our fortress, our refuge, our deliverer, and our all and in all. When we talk about a tower, we think about a tall, solid, and soaring kind of building, like that of a castle.

A tower in this context symbolizes different things such as: a fortified place of protection, safety and defense, a place of heights unknown, a place of soaring above all principalities, powers, and spiritual wickedness in heavenly realms, a place of favor, strength, and restoration. Christ Jesus, as our strong tower, reassures us that we are in a fortified place of protection and a place of safety from all the snares and fiery arrows of the enemy. In Him is a place of defense because the Lord Himself is our fortress and shield; He is our refuge, strength and helper when in trouble. *Therefore, we will not fear the waves and swaying of our boats (life's challenges), but we will stand tall and speak His Word to the giants that tend to revolt against us.* The Lord hides us under His mighty wings, where no weapons or schemes of the enemy against us shall succeed in our lives because the Lord almighty is with us and in us. The God of Abraham, Isaac, and Jacob is our refuge and our high tower.

Christ Jesus, our strong tower symbolizes *heights unknown.* When you are in Christ Jesus and He in you, He takes you on an adventure—to heights unknown. You begin to experience the impossible, the supernatural, through the working power of the Holy Spirit in you for His name's sake and glory. Christ Jesus mentioned, "Very truly I tell you, whoever believes in Me will do the works I have been doing, and they will do even greater things than these, because I am going to the Father." (John 14:12 NIV). Only trust and obey Him, who died for your redemption and rose again for your justification. He wants to do the mighty in you as your strong tower, and as our strong tower, we soar above every challenge the enemy throws at us. We are above all principalities, powers, rulers of the kingdom of darkness, and spiritual wickedness in heavenly realms. Therefore, if God is our God and He is always with us through His Holy Spirit, what harm can be against us and prevail? Trials and challenges will indeed come but they will never overcome us, since the Lord our God lives. He is our rock and our salvation; He is our fortress, and we will not be moved (Psalms 62:2 NIV).

Christ Jesus, our strong tower symbolizes a *place of favor.* When you are in Christ, His favor will go before you and be with you wherever He leads you. Amen! Just reflect on all of God's servants in the Bible—from Genesis to Revelation; His favor was manifested in their lives as they walked with Him. God's faithfulness towards you will never cease and His promises concerning you are forever and ever because of who He is and what He has done. As a child of God, you are like a tree planted by the streams of water, which yields its fruit in season and whose leaf does not wither, and whatever you do prospers (Psalms 1:3 NIV). The favor of the Lord shall be your portion when the Lord lives in you, and you abide in Him and in His Word.

Christ Jesus, our strong tower, is a *place of strength in times of weakness.* When you are weak, then you are strong because His strength is made perfect in your weakness. When you do not know which way to go, He is the way; and when all hopes are gone, that is when He has the perfect place to start in you. *He will take all your imperfections and make you perfect for His name's sake and glory; the Lord Jesus will build you, and you shall be built for His pleasure.* God's divine plan is established forever whether we are faithful or not; He is not slow in keeping His promises... instead He is patient with you and I, not wanting anyone to perish, but desires that everyone comes to repentance (2 Peter 3:9 NIV). Be still (wait on the Lord) and know that the Lord is God, and that His grace is sufficient for you because His promises are forever and ever, to those that love and trust in Him. Lay down all the worries, anxieties, pains, sicknesses, disappointments, and shame of this world at His feet, and He will give you rest and peace. The Word tells us that, "And we know that in all things God works for the good of those who love Him, who have been called according to His purpose." (Romans 8:28 NIV). He knows what is best for us and He always works everything out perfectly according to His Word and purpose in us. The Father loves us with an everlasting love through His Son Jesus Christ, so abide in His love through the power of His Word.

THE LOVE AND HEART OF THE FATHER

On one Christmas season, the Lord gave me this message, *"The love of the Father."* As I reflected on the birth of our Lord Jesus, the Holy Spirit made me to realize that creation, life, salvation, eternity, and all of existence, are because of the love of the Father. The Holy Spirit revealed to me that everything exists because of His love, and He wants us to open our eyes to this revelation of the importance of the love of the Father. It is a love that is so strong and powerful to the point of Him taking on flesh in the form of His one and only Son (Jesus Christ), to be a living sacrifice for humanity. Why would the Father and God of all things do such a thing? The answer is simple—*because of the love and heart of the Father.* The heart of the Father is not just a loving heart, but also a patient, merciful, and compassionate heart. The love of God is that aspect of His characteristics which made Him come down in the flesh to be an atonement for all sins of humanity. God does not want anyone to perish in Hell on that judgement day, which is why He came up with a plan to save us. Christ Jesus came in the flesh to live and experience life in the flesh; He suffered and died a terrible death because of love. Humans were separated from God due to our sinful nature and desires of their hearts; there was no way we could live sin free according to the standard of God the Father. The laws given to Moses were based on works and could not save people nor did the sacrificial blood of bulls take away sin permanently, until the sacrifice at calvary bore all sins away. Our Lord Jesus became the permanent atonement for sins once and for all because of the merciful and loving heart of the Father towards us. Forgiveness is costly, and a pure and holy sacrifice had to be made (shedding of blood and death) in place of the sinner (all of humanity). This demonstration of the loving heart of the Father for us clearly unveils that *love is indeed the centerpiece of God Himself,* and all of creation exists because of the love of the Father.

Christ Jesus has paid the ultimate price for our sins, so all you have to do is to confess your sins, ask for His forgiveness, and His Holy Spirit to come in and be the Lord of your heart. This is in accordance with His Word that, "If we confess our sins, He is faithful and just to forgive us our sins and purify us from all unrighteousness." (1 John 1:9 NIV). The blood of Christ Jesus purifies us from all sin (past, present, and future), and heals all our diseases—only if we believe and trust in Him. The heart of the Father is a heart of unfathomable patience—one that does not want any of His children to perish, but that all come to repentance (2 Peter 3:9 NIV). *So, if you hear His voice today, my friend, please, do not harden your heart; surrender to His call and will for your life, because if the Son sets you free, you will be free indeed from every chain that seems to bind you.* The Father's heart is always ready to take His children back regardless of our sins. Once we abide in Christ and He abides in us, and His Word abides in us, we become more like Him here on earth reflecting His mind, light, and Spirit through the power of the Holy Spirit in us.

Since we have been saved by grace through faith in our Lord Jesus Christ, let us grow in this grace and knowledge of Him, because the more we know Him, the better we can worship Him and have a relationship with Him. Let us press on to live a holy and godly lives in the mind and heart of the Father, as we await our Lord's second coming. Let us embrace this gift of salvation which was highly paid by the death of our Lord Jesus, all because of the heart of the Father. Some people have cast aside the Word of God and rejected His person and power; but our human hands or hearts *cannot remove or change the Lord God almighty nor His glory.* The Lord God can be denied, and His name even misused or usurped, but He cannot deny Himself; so, He remains faithful to His Word forever and ever. Amen! Let us continue to abide in His love, in His Word, and continue to follow His footsteps of righteousness until the day He comes, or the day we depart from this body and back into glory.

The Word of God tells us that, "Unless the LORD builds the house, they labor in vain who build it; unless the LORD guards the city, the watchman stays awake in vain." (Psalms 127:1 NKJV). We are the temple of the Lord because His Spirit dwells in us; hence, only He can build us and watch over us. We must commit our ways unto the Lord and trust in His Word and plan for our lives, even as His Spirit guides our hearts and minds. Christ is our source and the keeper of our souls, and to Him be all the glory, forever and ever! Amen. This is our reassurance: that He will always be there for us because He loves us unconditionally and eternally, and He is always ready to embrace us with loving-kindness, mercy, and grace when we return with a repentant heart. *There is nothing impossible in love, especially the love of the Father!*

Growing up as a child, I did not have the love of the father from my earthly father, so as a result, I clung to the love of my heavenly Father from a very early age. This relationship has and continues to be the most wonderful and precious thing in my journey of life. Without the love of our heavenly Father, one is certainly lost as you continuously seek love from the wrong things, places, and people. But when you realize and embrace the love of our heavenly Father, your life will never be the same. *Love, as you may know, is unexplainable and is far deeper than mere words; it is full of actions in demonstration of our emotions.* Love is not about our feeling as many may perceive it to be but rather our actions; actions that are much stronger and everlasting than our feelings—this is the love of the Father. As children of God, we are only responding to God's love for us through Christ Jesus, our Lord; the Father first loved us by making the first move towards us in love, mercy, and grace. Thus, let us not take God's loving-kindness for granted, but abide in His everlasting love through our actions of obedience to His Word. May the Lord bless and keep you, my dear friends, as you dwell in His presence, and may His Holy Spirit increase your love, wisdom, and revelation in the knowledge of Christ Jesus our Lord, in His mighty name. Amen!

THE POWER OF THE LOVE OF THE FATHER

Have you ever wondered why you are here, why you were born, or why God created everything including you in the first place? What motivated God to create everything in heaven and on earth, and under the earth? Again, the answer is plain and simple: Love, the love of God or the love of the Father. As we stated earlier, love is the centerpiece of God; everything came into existence out of love, and everything must be done in love. Whether it is works, faith, or even hope, it is all done due to the love of the Father that is shed abroad in our hearts. The Word of God tells us that, in the beginning, God created all things through His Son Jesus for His glory, and it was all very good. God also created people in His image and likeness and put them in charge of all that He had created (John 1:1–3; Genesis 1 NIV). The Father first loved us and had a plan for humanity even before the foundations of the world; He had a purpose for each person even before He formed us in the womb. Love is the motivating factor in all of creation because God is love; and when we develop this love in us, we reflect love Himself as God is love. This love of God in us must be spread to others like a sweet perfume; and anyone that loves not his fellow human being does not love God or know Him. At creation, God breathed the power of His breath into the first Adam and then he became alive, a living soul (Genesis 2:7 NKJV). This breath of God still sustains all people and all living things; and His Spirit still hovers over the face of the earth longing for a relationship with His children—all because of the love of the Father. There is power in God's love; it can cleanse the vilest or worst sinners, and make them whole and justified through the compassionate mercy of our Lord Jesus Christ. Amen! This agape kind of love can restore us back to the Father's arm through His saving grace, and can even heal our hopeless sicknesses and diseases through the precious blood of Christ Jesus our Lord.

We know that it is because of the power in God's love that moved Him to come up with a salvation plan for sin; yes, humans disobeyed God, and as a result, sin entered the world. The love of the Father compelled Him to make the first move towards us since we could not move towards Him due to our sins; our sins separated us from the love, presence, and security of God. It will take all eternity to thank God for His great love towards us through Christ Jesus, our Lord. The power of God's love for us moved Him to give us His best; such a powerful love that it forgives our sins and remembers them no more (Hebrews 8:12 NIV). The Father moved towards His beloved children in compassion regardless of our sins; He sent Christ Jesus to suffer and die, to take upon Himself our punishment, all because of love. Moreover, only Christ was worthy and without blemish to take away the sins of the world; no other sacrifice could take away human's sins forever. *Christ Jesus is the only atonement for sin—once and for all.* So, remember, my dear friends in the Lord, that it is no longer of good works that we are saved, but by grace through faith in what Christ Jesus has done. Our good works will *never* take the place of faith in God or our salvation, but good works, however, show forth our faith already placed in Christ. Good works would *never save* a person, but it is a fruit (action) of a saved life and shows forth the love of God. The Word of God tells us that Christ was doing good everywhere He went, mirroring the love of the Father in His actions. What is detesting in the sight of God is for people to do evil works and say they are doing the will of God; people doing all sorts of evil in the name of God and living lives that are quite contrary to God's Word and ways. If you are a Christian (Christ-like), your lifestyle must reflect that of Christ, you must do what is right in the sight of God and according to His Word, and your good works should show that your heart is right with the love of God. Then, you can go boldly in the presence of God, knowing fully well that Christ has paid the full penalty for your redemption, and your life is a living example of the power of His Word and Holy Spirit.

The things that we now do as we abide in God's love show forth our love and reverence for the Lord. As Christ Jesus said, "If you love Me, keep My commandments." (John 14:15 NKJV). In other words, do or obey the things that He has commanded you or the things you have heard or read in His Word and by His Holy Spirit. As we mentioned before, the power of love is far deeper than mere words. God's love was demonstrated in His *actions* towards us—from creation to the very works of Christ when He was on earth. The entire ministry of Christ on earth was ordained by the Father in love, in order to inspire our faith and reveal the Father unto us. Hence, we believe! There is nothing greater than the love of the Father, and this love is established forever, whether we remain faithful to God or not; God cannot deny Himself—He remains faithful in all His ways. God's love and Word remain eternal and trustworthy; so, let us abide in the power of His love, for there is great reward in doing so.

RESULT OF THE LOVE OF THE FATHER

The love of the Father towards His creation, especially the people He created, is immeasurable, unexplainable, and it comes with great reward. As already stated, we cannot understand why the God of the universe, the Father of life, the almighty, *all* powerful, and the great I am, would care so much for us. As believers in the Lord Jesus Christ, we must live in love and rely on the love that God has for us, which is in Christ Jesus our Lord. This is the confidence we have in Christ Jesus, that, "There is no fear in love. But perfect love drives out fear because fear has to do with punishment. The one who fears is not made perfect in love." (1 John 4:18 NIV). The love of God in us has set us free from all fear and bondage; this love of God is made complete in us in this life and throughout eternity. To the praise of His own glory! Amen.

In Christ and through faith in Him, we can now approach God with freedom and confidence, all because of His great love for us (Ephesians 3:12 NIV). It is the love of the Father that will cause God to honor His name by responding to our requests in prayer. Christ comforted His disciples saying, "And I will do whatever you ask in My name, so that the Father may be glorified in the Son. You may ask Me for anything in My name, and I will do it." (John 14:13–14 NIV). These same comforting words are also available for you and me today because of the love of the Father; ask the Father anything according to His Word, in His mighty name (the name of Jesus Christ), and He will give it to you, for His glory.

In Christ and through faith in Him, we now have the authority to do even greater things in His name through His Holy Spirit in us. Amen. The Holy Spirit in us is the seal of the Father's love for us, which is activated through our faith in Christ Jesus. Christ Jesus is now in the bosom of the Father (seated with the Father), where He was before taking on flesh; He is back to His dominion and majesty, and now intercedes on our behalf. All power in heaven, on earth, and under the earth, has been given to Him because of His obedience; therefore, every name or power is subjected under the name of Jesus Christ. *The name of Jesus Christ is the authority under which the true believer operates based on the Word of God.* For the joy that was set before Christ (the joy of our salvation), He became humble (enduring) and obedient to the will of God; therefore, the Father, who is a rewarder to those that do His will, gave Christ the highest reward:

> Therefore, God exalted Him to the highest place and gave Him the name that is above every name, that at the name of Jesus every knee should bow, in heaven and on earth and under the earth, and every tongue acknowledge that Jesus Christ is Lord, to the glory of God the Father. (Philippians 2:9–11 NIV).

As a result of our faith in Christ, we are now overcomers and victors over the schemes of the enemy because of the love of the Father. His Spirit is in us and we in Him, and His Word is us and active in us through the help of the Holy Spirit. That is why Christ said that, in this world we will face troubles, but we should not fear (we should be of good cheer) because He has overcome the world (John 16:33 NIV). Our peace lies in Christ, the peace that surpasses all human ideologies, understanding, and know-how. The favor of the Lord rests upon us wherever He leads us and in whatever we do. His Spirit guides and orders our every step along this lifelong journey in Christ, because in Him we live and have our entire existence. Our lives belong to the Lord and Him alone, for His pleasure and purpose, which is to have a true spiritual relationship with Him and worship Him in reverence and awe. The love of the Father keeps us from falling (into sin) since we are now slaves to righteousness and no longer slaves to sin in our minds and actions. We are now free like a bird from the snare of the devil, to serve our Lord and God! Our hearts are now right with the Lord through the power of the Holy Spirit; and as true children of God, we now seek to please the Father through the Son in all areas of our lives. We now live in Christ Jesus and in His powerful Word. We do not go back to our old ways (to the sinful desires of our hearts or flesh), but we are now led and controlled by the Spirit of God that lives in us. We are now a new creation in the mind of Christ, we are God's children born of the Spirit of God and heirs—heirs of God and co-heirs with Christ. Henceforth, my dear friends in the Lord, let us press on each day to lay hold of that eternal glory, to walk in the reality of Christ through His Word, and be the people that He has created us to be (to be all that He is). *No turning back!*

Let us abide in Him and manifest this love of the Father, which He has freely given to us as a gift, in all areas of our lives to the glory of God our Father. *There is nothing in this life that is greater and more fulfilling than the love of our heavenly Father, which is in Christ Jesus our Lord.* If we truly love the Lord God, let us with all sincerity abide in this great gift of His love by keeping His commands. May the love of the Father flood our hearts and minds more than the love of ourselves and of material things of this world, in the mighty name of Jesus Christ. Amen! Remember that Jesus Christ is the express image of the invisible God, the very essence of life, the Word of God that became flesh, and dwelt among us, full of grace and truth; Christ possesses all the fullness of the Father, the creator that became the creation, and He is the same yesterday, today, and forever. He changes not, and what He has done before He is still doing today and forevermore. He is the light of the world, the bread of life, the good shepherd, the rock, the gate, the resurrection, the vine, the way, the truth, the life of all living, and the sustainer of all created things, both great and small! Jesus Christ is above *all* things and over *all* things because He came from above, and in Him *all* things hold together. He is the first and the last, the alpha and the omega, the beginning, and the end; He is the Lord God almighty, the I am of the Old Testament. Jesus Christ is the covenant keeper because His Word stands forever, and it will never fail or return void. He is faithful to His Word and cannot deny Himself. He is the one the prophets spoke about—the savior of the world, our redeemer, and salvation. When you have the full revelation of Christ, you realize your identity and potential, since Christ is our blueprint and clear picture of our image. God has loved us with an everlasting love through our faith in Christ Jesus our Lord. He has given us His powerful and unchanging Word, and His Holy Spirit, which is our sword, weapon, and shield. So, my dear friends, *speak the Word of God into your lives today, declare the Word into your situation and stand on it in faith; do not look to the left or to the right in unbelief but have the eyes of faith and see what the loving Father sees because there is wonder working power in the spoken Word of God!*

3

THE SPOKEN WORD OF GOD

E very created thing whether great or small, visible or invisible, in heaven, on earth or under the earth, came into existence through the command of God the Father. There is supernatural power in the word of the sovereign God. The Word of God is God Himself, and it is so powerful that it surpasses every other power. God's Word has the power to create and give life to any dead situation; it refreshes, satisfies, and restores the human body and soul, giving joy to the heart, and light to the eyes. *The Word of God stands forever; it is perfect and trustworthy.* My dear friend, pay close attention to God's Word and your peace will be like a river, your well-being like the waves of the sea. Allow the Word of God into your soul, let it take root, and act upon it; it will prosper your soul. God's Word endures forever and will never return to Him void. There is power in the Word of God and power in the name of Jesus Christ our savior! *Whatever God says in His Word is final, and it settles every doubt when perceived through the eyes of the Father—through the eyes of faith.* Do not go by how you feel, by what you hear, or what you think about your present situation but go by what the Word of God says concerning you or that situation. Keep your eyes on the Lord Jesus and His Word and see those chains that tend to bind you fall off in the mighty name of Jesus Christ. Say what the Word says because there is power in the spoken Word of God!

The Word tells us that, all Scripture is God-breathed (from God) and is useful for teaching, rebuking, correcting, and training in righteousness, so that we (children or servants of God) may be thoroughly equipped for every good work (2 Timothy 3:16–17 NIV). God's Word is the pattern for God's children to follow; it is the way, the truth, and the life, as our Lord Jesus Christ clearly made it known. Commit your ways to the Lord because He is the way (the only true way); trust and rely totally on Him and not on your own ways and understanding. Creation came into existence by the spoken Word of God; likewise, as children of God, we should always declare the spoken Word of God into existence. The Word is our confirmation of what we believe; hence, we declare what we believe (the Word of God). Whatever you need in this life is found in the Lord Jesus Christ—in His Word through the power of His Holy Spirit. It does not matter what your circumstance or report may be, *there is nothing greater in this life than the creator of life itself—the Lord almighty, God.* A person is not limited in this life by anyone, anything, or their circumstances, but such is limited by the knowledge of the Word of God in them and their relationship with the Father. The mind of Christ in a person changes their perspective in every area of life. As a child of God, you understand through the help of the Holy Spirit that, no situation is beyond God's Word, His hand, (His reach) or power. Apostle Paul wrote through the Holy Spirit, "For the Word of God is living and powerful, and sharper than any two-edged sword, piercing even to the dividing of soul and spirit, and of joints and marrow, and is a discerner of the thoughts and intents of the heart." (Hebrews 4:12 NKJV). There is supernatural power in the spoken Word of God; it is so powerful to the pulling down of strongholds, to the dividing of the soul and the spirit, and even to the discerning of the thoughts and intents of our hearts.

Nothing or no creature is hidden from the sight of God, and there is certainly nothing too hard for the Lord God almighty, the creator and omniscient one; He certainly knows our deepest thoughts and secrets.

When you have a personal encounter with the Lord Jesus Christ, it changes everything in you; your life will never be the same. Wow! Paul experienced such greatness and power of God on his way to Damascus to persecute the Christians. During his journey, he had a life changing confront with the Lord Jesus Christ, that changed his life forever. He got to understand the power, mercy, faithfulness, and reality of the true living God in the face of Jesus Christ our Lord. As a result, Paul lived the rest of his life under the authority of the Lord Jesus through the Holy Spirit. He became a slave to righteousness, a slave to doing that which pleased the Lord Jesus according to the leadership of the Holy Spirit. When Christ becomes real in you, you not only allow His Word to take root in you but also act upon that Word through the help of His Spirit in you. I pray that every soul that reads this book would have a *personal encounter* with the Lord Jesus Christ through the power of the Holy Spirit; an encounter that will cause a supernatural change on the inside and out, to the glory of God. There is life changing power in the Word of God because everything came into existence through the spoken word or command of God, the Father.

Christians of today need to have the revelation of the *authority in the Word of God and believe what God has said in His Word (the Bible or Scriptures) in its entirety.* We must understand the power in the Word of God, which is the believer's guide in life, and weapon against every arrow of the enemy. Christ Jesus is that Word that became flesh and dwelt among us—the mystery and wisdom of God (John 1:14 NIV). The Word of God (Christ) is the light in your darkness and in your very life; it is a lamp for our feet, and a light on our paths (Psalms 119:105 NKJV). The living Word of God guides us into paths of righteousness, the right and only way to go; the Word gives us wisdom, direction, reassurance, comfort, faith, joy, and peace that surpasses all human knowledge and understanding. When God's Word enters the heart of a person, it brings forth light in their soul, and its unfolding gives comprehension of the knowledge of God (Psalms 119:130 NKJV). The spoken Word of God is life, it has the power to create and resurrect hopeless situations, and impossibilities become possible because of the power in the Word of God. God's Word is eternal, it stands forever, and will never return to Him void, but will forever do exactly that for which it was sent forth to do, to the glory and pleasure of the Father (Isaiah 55:10–11 NIV). From now on, view the Word of God as the power and source of all life; that power which holds *all* things together. Thus, whatever the Word says concerning any situation is final; just believe in the Word and stand on it because God does not deny Himself. Man does not have the final answers; neither our doctors, nor our lawyers, or even any of us have the answers to our circumstances, but the Lord God has the final word about our lives. He wonderfully created us and weaved together every fiber of our being; amazingly and perfectly made us for a great work in Him. So, allow His plan according to His Word and Holy Spirit to rule and reign in you because you belong to Him—you are His.

What God has said before, still stands even today because His character and nature do not change. God's divine Word is forever, since whatever is now has already been, and what will be has been before (Ecclesiastes 3:15 NIV). There is nothing new under the heavens, and everything is only temporal and will surely pass away, but the Word of the Lord endures forever. Be rest assured when you declare the Word of God as He is ready to perform it, not because of you but for who He is, and what He has done. It is never about us but all about Him, and Him alone. God is His Word—unchangeable, powerful, creative, and infallible; it is trustworthy, reliable, just, and endures forever. Before God speaks any word, He first has a clear imagination, a visual image in His mind before He declares it. He sees the product in His mind with the eyes of faith (in the spiritual realm) before it becomes a spoken word. Likewise, as children of God, settle the battle first in your mind, see that problem solved, that sickness healed, that pain gone in your mind before declaring the Word of God. Have the eyes of faith like the Father, believing in every Word that He has spoken, in the mighty name of Jesus Christ. Since God's Word is life itself, when it is spoken, it creates and brings into being. The Bible is God's spoken creative Word, and when it enters the good soil of a heart, the right ground and takes root, it then produces much fruit. God is perfect from the beginning, and is perfect now and forever, and so is His spoken Word. Human progresses from cradle till death, but God does not; He remains the same. We are only discovering God in our day and dispensation. God does not have a better way of doing things; He is perfect and in Him there is no imperfection or darkness. The Lord has loved us just the way we are, but He perfects us once we are in Him, in order to be more like Him through the power of His Holy Spirit.

When we put our faith in God's Word—in His spoken Word, impossible things become possible; healing for example, becomes simple. *When we focus our thoughts on the fact that everything that God has said and done is complete, that every Word of God is already established, then we begin to see the supernatural come to pass in the mighty name of Jesus Christ.* In the Old Testament, God spoke to the prophets, and the prophets took the message to the people saying, "Thus saith the Lord" and the Lord God was with them, bringing to pass every Word He had spoken. The Father is still speaking directly to His people and honoring every spoken Word. He speaks to His children through the ministry of Christ Jesus, and in these last days, God speaks through His Holy Spirit since the day of Pentecost. We have the same power and message of the Word, to go into all the world in the mighty name of Jesus Christ, to declare His truth, to take authority over the works of the enemy (to bind and loose), and it shall be done through the power of His Holy Spirit in us. As children of God, we are sent to the world to heal every manner of disease, to set the captives free, and heal the broken hearted in the mighty name of Jesus Christ. It is not about us or in our own power, but it is all about Christ and in His power (the power of His Holy Spirit), for His glory; we are only obedient vessels for the Lord. When we get to that point of faith, every doubt and fear is taken away, and every Word of God is perfected with great signs and wonders in His mighty name. Allow the Holy Spirit of God to guide you into all truth and He will be glorified in you.

Be patient my dear friends, believing that whatever you declare according to the Word of God has the power to come to pass. Do not allow your present circumstance to determine your life; your life is determined by the Word of God in you and your relationship with Him. As stated earlier, one is only limited by the knowledge of the Word in you, limited by the Word, and your relationship with the Lord Jesus. *So, be patience as you wait on the Lord in prayer and never give in or surrender to your circumstances because your present situations do not determine who you are or limit you; rather, stand firm in your faith in Christ Jesus and His Word, and do not waver in your faith until the very end.* Positive words out of your mouth based on God's Word will make your way prosperous; a changed mind in Christ leads to a successful life in Him. Let your words agree with what you desire; let your words agree with God's Word concerning your situation. Do not be moved by what you see, feel, hear, or your situation, only be moved by God's Word and your faith. See things the way God see them, and do not conform or go by the pattern of this world—the way the world sees things. The Word of God is the evidence to the eyes of your faith and never your circumstances. Say to the devil, "It is written." In the gospel of Matthew, Christ said, "It is written: 'Man shall not live on bread alone, but on every word, that comes from the mouth of God." (Matthew 4:4 NIV). If our Lord Jesus defeated the devil through the Word, so must we. It is *only* through the Word of God and the name of Jesus Christ that we can overcome the kingdom of darkness or this world, including every principality, power, or spiritual wickedness in high places.

The words you speak portray who you are—portray your life, your character, your faith, and your hope. What comes out of your mouth has the power to heal, create, restore, as well as the power to destroy, or kill. Let the supernatural power of God depart from your mouth as instructed by the Father, so that you will live the life that God intended you to live (righteous, prosperous, and abounding life in every way). God searches and knows the deepest thoughts and plans of your heart that no one knows. God's Word judges the thoughts and attitudes of our hearts; it convicts our hearts of any sin and reveals Christ Jesus to us when His Word is deeply rooted in our hearts, causing us to act upon it. For us to operate fully in the power of the Word of God, we must establish a relationship with the Word Himself (Christ Jesus). We must surrender our lives to the Lord for all that He has done for us especially on the cross for our sins through His sacrificial atonement. Through His death and resurrection, Christ has given us the authority over the kingdom of this world through the power of His Word; God has freely given us the authority on this earth, and He honors His name and Word forever. It was the same authority the Father gave to Adam and Eve in the Garden of Eden, but this authority was handed over to the devil through disobedience. Christ Jesus has bought that authority back by His precious blood shed on the cross. So, if you love the Lord Jesus, obey His Word; your love for the Lord God must be sincere. Hate what is evil and cling to that which is good and pleasing in the sight of God (Romans 12:9 NIV). There was no conqueror before Christ and there is none beside Him; He alone is the savior, the redeemer, and the only God and Lord, Jesus Christ is His name. The authority has been given to those that believe and trust in Him; through the name of Jesus Christ, to command and change whatever may come our way according to His Word. Submit yourself in faith to the Lord, then resist the devil by speaking the Word of God in the mighty name of Jesus, and the devil has no choice but to flee from you (James 4:7 NKJV).

A life lived by faith and in love of God's Word will also be a prosperous life full of joy and peace in the Lord Jesus. You cannot say you are a child of God or a believer but act contrary to what His Word says. Our actions show forth who we truly are—a child of God or not. As children of God, the fruits (evidence) of God or of the Holy Spirit must be clearly seen in us and through us in all areas of our lives. We must have a passion for the things of God, which starts with faith in His Word. Faith in the Word of God is fundamental in our relationship with God because it is impossible to live a successful Christian life without faith in the Word of God. It is in the Word, and from the Word that we find the solution to every situation because Christ Jesus is our source. God is far greater and bigger than any problem you would ever have; no problem is too big to stop God's plan for your life; He had a purpose for your life even before He formed you in the womb. The creator of *all* things is in control of your life—"What is impossible with man, is possible with God." (Luke 18:27 NIV). Nevertheless, God will sometimes allow things to happen to His children, to get our attention when we are detouring from His will; and moreover, these challenges bring us into fellowship with God and build our faith, hope, and trust in Him. Pure love includes correction and in return for God's enduring love, people ought to obey His Word, have a life that is totally submissive and devoted to Him and the Word—a lifestyle that ascribes glory due to God. Such a lifestyle puts a smile on the face of the Lord and brings one everlasting joy and peace. Let us not allow sin in our lives to rob us of God's fellowship and blessings. The more we give ourselves to God, the more God is willing to give Himself to us; it is a choice to either accept and follow the Lord Jesus or not. *It is not until you die to yourself (totally committed), not until you die to the sinful desires of your flesh, that you truly come alive and be the person God created you to be.* God is looking for a willing and obedient heart and a vessel to use; a vessel He can work through for His glory and praise.

It is the Word of God that convicts the heart unto salvation through the power of the Holy Spirit at work in that person. It is a conviction that comes only through the power in the Word of God leading to total surrender and obedience to God's purpose for your life. As a child of God through faith in Christ Jesus, the *Word of God is our all and in all—our manual for life. A life fed with the Word of God is a life that is born of the Spirit of God; one that seeks after the heart of God through the help of the Spirit of God. Such a life is in total submission to the leadership, guidance, voice, and revelation of the Spirit of God.* Have faith in God's Word, for the answer is, *just have faith!* All things are possible to those that are His, those that believe in the Lord Jesus, and to them that dwell in Him through His Word and His Spirit! The Word of God is powerful and will never fail those that trust in Him and walk in it. God's Word breaks every chain and sets free every captive. The Lord has never stopped loving you because He has loved you with an everlasting love. Remember God's Word to the prophet Isaiah saying, "The grass withers and the flowers fall, but the Word of our God endures forever." (Isaiah 40:8 NIV). Again:

> As the rain and the snow come down from heaven,
> and do not return to it without watering the earth
> and making it bud and flourish, so that it yields
> seed for the sower and bread for the eater, so is
> My word that goes out from My mouth: it will
> not return to Me empty but will accomplish what
> I desire and achieve the purpose for which I sent
> it. (Isaiah 55:10–11 NIV).

Remember that every Word of God you declare with all conviction, boldness, and awe in the mighty name of Jesus Christ, shall surely come to pass. "God is not human that He should lie, not a human being, that He should change His mind. Does He speak and then not act? Does He promise and not fulfill?" (Numbers 23:19 NIV). There is power in every spoken Word of God!

At all times and in everything that you do, stand on what the Word of God says; do not go by what you see, hear, feel, or know. Always ask yourself, "What does the Word of God says concerning this situation?" For example: 'The Lord is my healer,' because according to Exodus 15:26, the Lord says, "...I am the Lord who heals you." (Exodus 15:26 NIV), "...The joy of the Lord is my strength." (Nehemiah 8:10 NIV). Then start to ponder upon that Word of God, applying the Word to yourself personally, knowing fully well that God is still the same and so is His Word. *God's Word then, still applies to us today; what He spoke to the Israelites then, still applies to us as His children today because God's Word changes not, and no situation is new under the heavens.* Begin to see things the way God sees them—see victory! Out of the abundance of the Word of God in you, speak to that mountain in your life in the mighty name of Jesus Christ our Lord. Walk in the reality of the authority He has given to us through His Holy Spirit in us. Hence, bind what you do not want to see in your life and loose that which you want to see happen according to the Word of God in the mighty name of Jesus Christ. When you spend time with the Lord in fellowship, prayer, and in His Word, you will come to understand your identity, and His perfect will for your life through the power of His Holy Spirit. There is power in the name of Jesus Christ!

THERE IS POWER IN THE NAME OF JESUS

My earnest prayer is that one day all believers in Christ Jesus will come to the full *knowledge and revelation of the power in the name of Jesus Christ.* The authority in the name of Jesus Christ behind those that believe in Him, is far greater and more powerful than any other powers. The power in the name of Jesus Christ is from above and above *all* other powers; and this is the power behind every believer, to do whatsoever according to God's will (Matthew 28:18 NIV). The name of Christ Jesus is the doctor in the sickroom, the judge in the courtroom, the counselor in your marriage, the restorer of your family, the mediator, the comforter, the life, and your all and in all. The name of Christ Jesus is the mighty tower, and the righteous and sinners run into it and are safe from their enemies. The name of Jesus Christ is the believer's weapon, that breaks every yoke and shackle of the devil in our lives. The name of Christ Jesus is the light of all humanity and the source of life itself. He promised, saying, "... whatever you ask in My name the Father will give you." (John 15:16 NIV). The name of Jesus Christ is freely given from the moment a person repents and accepts Christ as the Lord of their life. Thus, use the Word and the name of Jesus Christ in all areas of your life; only believe in Him with every fiber of your being, and speak the Word of God in His name, standing on the truth that, there is power in the spoken Word of God.

There is power in the name of Christ Jesus because He is the living Word of God that became flesh and dwelt among us. Christ was with God in the beginning, and through Him were all things created at the command of the Father (John 1:2 NIV). He came to fulfill the promise of a savior that was prophesied to the prophets throughout the generations—the savior that will reconcile people back to God, and reveal the love and mercy of the Father to the world. Once again, the Father stepped down to us but this time in the flesh to save those in the flesh from their sins—*the creator became the created.* God stepped into time, lived a perfect life, and humbled Himself unto death even death on the cross for you and me, and all that would receive Him. Jesus Christ paid for all our sins and gave us His Holy Spirit to be with us forever. The gift of salvation is free to anyone who accepts Jesus Christ as their Lord and savior. He then offers the gift of living a quality life in Him (eternity) through His Holy Spirit and His Word. *Remember that your life is a gift from God, you did not ask for it, so it belongs to Him; and what you do with the gift of your life is also your gift in return to God.* Do not live your life anyhow but be intentional, knowing fully well that you belong to God, and that you will give an account of your life when you stand before the Lord on judgement day. When you abide in the Word, you begin to enjoy fellowship with the Lord Jesus Christ continually, and eventually it becomes a lifestyle and a sweet savor.

Christ Jesus is *real, and so is His Word and His Holy Spirit.* Thus, Christianity is an authentic way of life and a relationship with the Father, our creator and sustainer of our being. Here is how the apostle John described the revelation of Christ and His being:

> The hair on His head was white like wool, as white as snow, and His eyes were like blazing fire. His feet were like bronze glowing in a furnace, and His voice was like the sound of rushing waters. In His right hand He held seven stars, and coming out of His mouth was a sharp, double-edged sword. His face was like the sun shining in all its brilliance. (Revelation1:14–16 NIV).

The two-edged sword out of His mouth signifies the 'Word of God', since Christ is also called the 'Word of God'—the name given to Him by the Father (Revelation 19:13 NIV). Just imagine how John felt seeing the glory of the living God; like all others before him, he could not withstand the brilliance of the Lord's appearance and so falls facedown, as though dead, in reverential fear and awe. Envision God, the creator of *all* things, standing right before John, revealing to him things that were to take place before the great day of the Lord, when Christ will descend back on the earth the same way He ascended into heaven. What a glorious day it will be! All eyes will see Him, even those that crucified Him according to the revelator. Christ Jesus is as real as the air we breathe and so is His Word. Declare His Word with all confidence, wavering not in unbelief in His mighty name; and be still, knowing fully well that there is supernatural power in the spoken Word of God.

BE STILL AND KNOW THAT I AM GOD

Our focus as children of God must be to know who God is, to be still in His presence, to seek His face, and be absolutely persuaded about His power, might, and sovereignty. Even as we are determined to know God by seeking Him through His Word and His face in prayer, God in return is continuously in the process of changing us day by day through His eternal works in us. We need to know that God is God, and that it is He who has made us in love, and not we ourselves; we did not ask to be born but God in His love wonderfully knit us together in our mother's womb. God is the *only* magnificent, powerful, sovereign, awesome, great, and mighty God, and He deserves all our praise and adoration! King Solomon's teachings in Ecclesiastes 3 are powerfully transforming. He declared that no one could add anything to what God is doing, what He has done, and no one can take anything from it (Ecclesiastes 3:14 NIV). It is all about God, and for Him! This truth about God brings us to worship and awe of Him. The Bible enlightens us that Christ Jesus called His disciples to walk with Him and the disciples obeyed Him, and His life and Spirit abided in them. When the Word of God and the life of God abides in us, He will fulfill His works through us. Apostle Paul in the letter to the Ephesians confirms this truth that: "For we are His workmanship, created in Christ Jesus for good works, which God prepared beforehand, that we should walk in them." (Ephesians 2:10 NKJV). God, through Christ, has called us to walk in the works He has prepared for us even before He created us. The questions we are faced with are: Why do we look for answers everywhere else before looking up to Christ Jesus? Why do we shift our focus and put our trust in the things God has created rather than trusting God our creator? God is clearly and constantly telling us to be still and know that He is God, and that He will be exalted in the nations and in the earth (Psalms 46:10 NKJV). No matter the mayhem going on in our lives, in our societies, in our communities, or the world at large; just be still and keep your eyes on the Lord Jesus because heaven still rules, and God is still supreme over *all*. God created all things through Christ, and He owns everything. God's strength is made perfect in our weakness, no matter how low we may go; His Word is more powerful than any other powers. Apostle Paul's journey in the Lord was a typical example of God's grace and mercy upon His children. He states in his dialogue with the Lord in 2 Corinthians 12:

> But He said to me, "My grace is sufficient for you, for My power is made perfect in weakness. Therefore, I will boast all the more gladly about my weaknesses, so that Christ's power may rest on me. That is why, for Christ's sake, I delight in weaknesses, in insults, in hardships, in persecutions, in difficulties. For when I am weak, then I am strong. (2 Corinthians 12:9–10 NIV).

When we are weak, then we are strong because God's grace through Christ (the grace that does not look back to our past sins) is sufficient for us. There is no problem that is above God or too big for Him; no mountain is too high for Him. All powers in heaven and earth belong to God, and He has given us that authority in His name over every other power. Hence, Paul was able to boast in His weaknesses because it was an opportunity for God to be glorified through him. God watches over us (His children), He delights in us and He loves us so much! All we must do is to be still and know that He is God through our faith in Christ Jesus.

When we surrender our lives to the Lord Jesus, He forgives our sins and we become slaves to righteousness through the power and strength of His Holy Spirit. The love of Christ in us through our rebirth, compels us to seek after righteousness in the Lord, and this becomes our new identity and lifestyle in Him, through the help of the Holy Spirit. We must come before the Lord with a responsive heart, abiding, and sharing the life of the Father through His Son. He then pours His life through us in the fulfillment of His will. *The key to life and any work of God is not who we are, and certainly not what we are able to do. The key is who Christ Jesus is and what He can do in us and through us. Christ is our only hope in life, our hope in His work given to us, and certainly our hope in our relationships.* We must place our hope in Christ (who draws people to Himself) rather than in our own abilities and knowledge; we must turn continually to God for what He will do rather than trust in ourselves and others. Such a relationship with God brings fruitfulness in us; you must know whom you have believed and be at peace in Him no matter the challenges of this world. Our reassurance lies in our faith in the entirety of God's Word, and here is an example of God's reassurance to those that love Him:

> Whoever dwells in the shelter of the Most High
> will rest in the shadow of the Almighty. I will say
> of the LORD, "He is my refuge and my fortress,
> my God, in whom I trust." Surely, He will save
> you from the fowler's snare and from the deadly
> pestilence. He will cover you with His feathers,
> and under His wings you will find refuge; His
> faithfulness will be your shield and rampart. You
> will not fear the terror of night, nor the arrow that
> flies by day, nor the pestilence that stalks in the
> darkness, nor the plague that destroys at midday.

A thousand may fall at your side, ten thousand at your right hand, but it will not come near you. You will only observe with your eyes and see the punishment of the wicked. If you say, "The LORD is my refuge," and you make the Most High your dwelling, no harm will overtake you, no disaster will come near your tent. For He will command His angels concerning you to guard you in all your ways; they will lift you up in their hands, so that you will not strike your foot against a stone. You will tread on the lion and the cobra; you will trample the great lion and the serpent. "Because He loves me," says the LORD, "I will rescue him; I will protect him, for he acknowledges My name. He will call on Me, and I will answer him; I will be with him in trouble, I will deliver him and honor him. With long life I will satisfy him and show him My salvation. (Psalms 91 NIV).

Be still and know that He is God and that His strength is made perfect in your weaknesses; the Lord is faithful to every Word! The Word of God tells us in Genesis that:

In the beginning God created the heavens and earth. Now the earth was formless and empty, darkness was over the surface of the deep, and the Spirit of God was hovering over the waters. And God said, "Let there be light," and there was light. God saw that the light was good, and He separated the light from the darkness. God called the light "day," and the darkness He called "night." And there was evening, and there was morning—the first day. (Genesis 1:1–5 NIV).

We can see that there was total darkness, confusion, and mayhem going on upon the formless earth. Then the voice of the Lord God declared; He commanded saying, "Let there be..." What happened when God spoke? Things began to manifest by the power of His Word—yes, indeed! Every Word that God declared came into existence; light appeared according to the authority in His Word, and so did every other thing, under the sound of God's voice. Likewise, we have the same Word of God as children of God; so, let us use it in every area of our lives, to the glory of God, the Father. We have been separated from the kingdom of this world to God's kingdom through faith in our Lord Jesus Christ, and Christ has also given us the authority of His name to destroy, pull down, bind, and lose all works of the enemy. Everything God commanded came into being without doubting His Words; everything stood firm out of things that were *unseen, and His commandments still stand today and forever.* Since we were created in the image and likeness of God, we possess the qualities of our creator because we have now been reconciled with God through faith in Christ Jesus, and His Holy Spirit is at work in us and through us via His Word. Henceforth, let us declare what we have already seen in the spiritual realm into the physical in the name of Jesus Christ. We know now that God began with the Word, so we must start with His Word. Amen!

My pastor once said that, "Knowing and not doing, is not knowing at all." Know that the moment you repent of your sins and make the Lord Jesus *"The Boss"* over your life, you become a child of the living God (saved or born again); from henceforth you belong to the kingdom of God. Outside of the knowledge of the almighty God people are destroyed. When God's people neglect and reject the ways of the Lord, they fall away from the protection of the Father and are given over to depraved spirits, and fall under the wrath of God. Staying under the shelter of the Lord through faith in Christ, in His Spirit and in His Word, set you free from the kingdom of this dark world; the truth of the Word is what sustains and sets you free as you stand on it. Faith in the Lord yields forth fruits of the Spirit of God in you and through you; and these are manifested in every aspect of your life. *But knowing is not just enough, you need to act on what you know in all areas of your life.* Acting on what you know as a believer in the Lord Jesus Christ is the evidence of your faith, and it is a new way of living, your old way of living is dead. As a child of God, you cannot continue in your old sinful ways because the grace of God is freely available. You have been saved by His precious grace, so you live in His salvation with all fear and trembling according to His Word and Spirit. The Holy Spirit of God living in you helps you on this new journey of life through your faith in Christ Jesus and His Word. Just as it is written, "The righteous will live by faith." (Romans 1:17 NIV). Stand on the authority that Christ has freely given to you when you became a child of God. "For no matter how many promises God has made, they are "Yes" in Christ. And so, through Him the "Amen" is spoken by us to the glory of God." (2 Corinthians 1:20 NIV). Be mindful that the enemy will always try to distract us from following the ways of God; he will even come up with a substitution for the Word of God, or simply try to turn the Word of God against us. This was evidenced in the Garden of Eden, where Satan deceived Eve by turning the Word of God against her and creating doubt (Genesis 3:1–6 NIV). But we know that the devil is the greatest liar and the most cunning creature ever! Whatever God says in His Word concerning you is *final*—no one and not even the devil or anything, can stop it! *If the Word of God says, you are blessed, healed, sanctified, strong, loved, and filled with His power, then, that is what it is.* Stand firm on the true Word of God with no shadow of doubt, believing that whatever you declare in the powerful name of Jesus Christ will surely come to pass. *Faith is the victory that overcomes the world; our faith in God's Word and in what He has done is our weapon and victory.*

God's faithfulness to all His creation is from generation to generation, and He watches over them. To name a few examples of God's faithfulness that we take for granted: There is still air for all to breathe (for both the good and the bad), the seasons still change upon the face of the earth, the shrubs and plants still grow at their appointed time, and all living things still reproduce after their kind and fill the earth at their appointed time, because God's commandments stand forever. Everything God has created and put in place exemplify His glory, greatness, and the reality of who He is. Apostle Paul revealed such in Romans, "For since the creation of the world, God's invisible qualities—His eternal power and divine nature have been clearly seen, being understood from what has been made, so that people are without excuse." (Romans 1:20 NIV). Yes, humans have no excuse for not serving, glorifying, and reverencing their creator and sustainer, whose faithfulness is abundant unto all His creation. God has revealed Himself in all that He has created, in His Word, and through His Son Jesus Christ; and once more, God has revealed Himself through His Holy Spirit who the world struggles to accept because they neither see Him or know Him; but we (the children of God) know Him because He lives with us and in us (John 14:17 NIV). As stated earlier, *serving God is a reality, and His Spirit is real; it is not a religion but a way of life, a relationship with the Father, and the will of the Father for us.*

The Word of God and God Himself are the same—faithful and true. The Word illuminates our darkness, bringing light into our paths; it creates and gives life to hopeless situations because the Lord Jesus is the living Word and the light of the world. If you believe in Him and His Word, you will never be part of this dark world, but will have the light, which is His life. All you need to do now is, believe God's Word, claim it, and receive it, in the mighty name of Jesus Christ. When God looks upon you, He sees the blood of Christ; He does not see the old you in your sinful ways any longer, but He sees the redeemed, sanctified, and renewed child of God, born of His Spirit. *Christ Jesus is our identity!* When you have the full knowledge of Christ, you discover your identity and blueprint. Consequently, when people see you, they should see Christ Jesus in you and through you—in all aspect of your life. Your life must reflect that of your Father and His image and character; your life must mirror *all the fruits of His Spirit in you, namely: Love, joy, peace, patience, kindness, goodness, faithfulness, gentleness, and self-control (Galatians 5:22-23 NIV).* Then you will be able to overcome the challenges of this dark world through living and declaring the Word of God; being certain that God is faithful to every Word He has spoken. God and His Word are inseparable. Jesus Christ is the Word of God, and He also revealed this revelation clearly to His disciples saying, "I and the Father are one." (John 10:30 NIV). He also mentioned that "… Anyone who has seen Me has seen the Father. Don't you believe that I am in the Father, and that the Father in Me?" (John 14:9–10 NIV). Also, "If you remain in Me and My words remain in you, ask whatever you wish, and it will be done for you. This is to My Father's glory, that you bear much fruit, showing yourselves to be My disciples." (John 15:7–8 NIV). Christ is in the Father and the Father is in Him; He is the one and same God, and He remains faithful. So, declare the life changing Word of God into your life today and stand on the reality of Christ Jesus our Lord!

I AM THE LORD

The Lord reminded me once more as I waited on Him in worship with this statement, "I have heard your cry and have come down because I am the Lord." Many a times we feel as though the Lord has turned His face away from us and gone completely silent to our plea, but His Word is that He has heard every cry and petition, and He has now come in power and might (through His Holy Spirit), to restore His people back to Himself. Yes, sometimes the Lord will hide His face from us due to our disobedience and sinful ways, but when we return to His presence in surrender and repentance, He moves once more towards us in forgiveness. No matter what you are going through or what your present situation may be, there is a day that your cry will reach before the Lord, and He will come down (through His Word and His Holy Spirit) to see if the situation is as bad as the outcry that has reached before Him. We also evidenced such in the outcry against Sodom and Gomorrah in Genesis 18:20. The Father is not only a merciful God, but He is also a just king, and when we abide in the Lord and He abides in us and His Word abides in us, He honors us by honoring every Word of God we declare.

For Moses to have a relationship with God, he had to have the revelation of the knowledge of God, so, the Father revealed His identity to him in Exodus saying, "...I am who I am." (Exodus 3:14 NKJV). In other words, God will be whosoever and whatsoever He desires to be. There is no limit to His sovereignty and power; He is the Lord. He created all things, and hence, He is above all things. He is the beginning and the end of everything, the alpha and the omega, and the mighty one; there is no God besides Him, and apart from Him there is no other. Rest in His peace, my dear friends!

THE GOSPEL IS NOW

Every word, revelation, promise, or situation written in the Scriptures, not only spoke to those before us, but also speaks to you and me today and forever more. Every Word of God applies to us, to our generation, our day and our time, too. The Word of God is still alive, active, powerful, and unchanging, forever more. God's character, which is in His Word, does not change; He is His Word, and His Word is trustworthy. His Spirit is the only person who can reveal this mystery to us, and this is the reason why we cannot do the work of God without the leadership of the Holy Spirit. We cannot worship God without His Spirit because God is a 'Spirit.' Hence, Christianity without the Holy Spirit is no Christianity at all but dead religion! Christ Jesus did not only die on the cross and rose again on the third day just to cover your sins and bring you eternal life. He did not die so we can continue living in our bondage of sickness, poverty, pain, depression, darkness, fear, mourning, sadness, and confusion. Christ Jesus died so that we may live more abundantly to the glory of the God the Father. Every word, every promise, and every revelation in God's Word is for you and me today; God has not changed and neither has His ways, nor His Word. All you have and need is your faith in Christ Jesus to overcome your world; claim that Word of God concerning your life and fully walk in it without turning to the left or to the right. *Faith is right now!* It was not only for our fellow brethren, or for the future, but the Word is also for the *now!*

Christ Jesus is the same today, and He changes not. He promised that whatever we ask in His name He will do it, so that the Father may be glorified in the Son (John 14:13 NIV). *Whatever means whatever; not just some things, but whatsoever you surrender to Him!* Christ Jesus does not just want you to enjoy life when you get to heaven, He wants you also to live to the full even right here on earth; that is why He came, so that His children will live more abundantly, and give Him all the glory. Christ came to preach the good news of salvation to all, including the meek, afflicted, and the poor in spirit. He came to bind up and heal, to proclaim freedom (physical and spiritual freedom) for the captives, to release from darkness those that are in prison (in their minds), to open the blind eyes (physical and spiritual blindness), and He came to also comfort (Isaiah 61 NIV). The gospel is now, and it is for you and me, for our generation and our time; what the Lord has done before, He can do even greater now. Every promise of the Lord is active and powerful and is for us today as children of God; children born of the Spirit of God through the precious blood of Christ Jesus. Do not allow the enemy, the devil through his scheme of guilt, to rob you of what God has freely given you through faith in Christ Jesus our Lord.

GUILT—THE ENEMY'S SCHEME

Is guilt having its way in your life? Have you forgotten who you are, whose you are, and what has been done for you? As we talked earlier, do not allow the enemy to rob you (through his scheme of guilt and doubt), of what God has freely given His children. Guilt is one form of the enemy's schemes and lies but remember that as children of God we have received the Holy Spirit of God, the Spirit of power, love, and of a sound mind, and not a spirit of confusion, lie, anxiety, or fear. God's Spirit in us is far greater and powerful than every lying spirits out there because we now live in the Spirit, love and mind of Christ Jesus our Lord. Satan would try to make you believe that your sins have not been forgiving even after accepting the Lord Jesus as your savior; He creates doubts in the minds of God's children, because he is the greatest liar and deceiver ever. For example, "Has God really forgiven all of your sin?" This could be one of the doubts the enemy keeps telling you. But remember that Jesus' sacrifice on the cross took away all our sins, and we are to live no more in fear but in victory. "For you did not received the Spirit of bondage again to fear, but you received the Spirit of adoption by whom we cry, "Abba Father." (Romans 8:15 NKJV). Continue to keep your eyes on the Lord and obey His Word. Meditate on His Word and allow the Word to be embedded in your soul; so that you will know Him better, worship Him the right way, know who you are in Him, and understand your inheritance in Him. It is only through the Word of God that we can defeat the lies of Satan, because of the power in the name of Jesus and His Word. God will never forsake His children, His promise, and His covenant of love; He is forever faithful because His name is faithful and true.

THERE IS HOPE IN SILENCE
AND HOPELESSNESS

During the winter season, everything appears dead and without hope. One morning, as I watched out of my kitchen window, I was marveled once again at the glory of God displayed in the silence in the atmosphere; silence brought about by the cold winter weather. The Lord reminded me through His Holy Spirit that, "There is hope in silence and hopelessness." Have you ever felt a *sense of silence* in your life? Oh yes! I believe we have all felt like this at some point in our lives. These false feelings or lies come from the greatest liar of all—the devil known as Satan. Do not give in to these lies because what the Word of God says concerning you is the only truth that you must adhere to as a child of God. Christ Jesus is our only hope even in our silence and hopeless situations. God's Word does not *die or expire* but remains powerful, unchanging, and full of life. On that beautiful morning, the Holy Spirit opened my spiritual eyes to realize that there is a time and a season for everything; I realized that springtime is a perfect display of God's potential in everything He has created. From what seems to be hopeless and dead during the winter months, to new life springing forth in the season of spring. That situation that seems hopeless, my dear friends, has the power, potential, and ability to change, grow, restore, re-create, come alive, and do well in the mighty name of Jesus Christ and according to His Word. Out of the ashes of winter, beauty springs forth all around us and in the atmosphere during the springtime. Even though the winter months come with silence, silence does not mean death, no hope, and no restoration. *Silence is a preparation period for the beautiful and great things God is about to birth forth in us.* Silence unlocks God's power because He is always at work, even though you might not notice or see it. "He has made everything beautiful in its time. He has also set eternity in the human heart; yet no one can fathom what God has done from beginning to end." (Ecclesiastes 3:11 NIV). There is life in that challenge that seems dead and hopeless, there is healing power in that sick body, and restoration in that situation in the mighty name of Jesus. There is a God-given potential and hunger in your soul that only God can satisfy and fulfill through faith in Him. Just align yourself with the Lord Jesus, wait on Him through His Word and Spirit, and believe that whatsoever He has said in His Word, He will surely do.

We have hope even though we are living at a very crucial time; living in a world that is full of all sorts of wickedness and evil in every way. But we thank God that even though we are in this world, we are no more of it, no more of its image and pattern of things. Christ Jesus has delivered us from the kingdom of this world through the redemption and forgiveness of our sins on the cross, and He has brought us into His marvelous light, into His kingdom (Colossians 1:13–14 NIV). It is only through Christ Jesus, the Word of God and the Holy Spirit that we can overcome the evil and be saved. When the world says, *'you are no good;' tell the world, 'I am blessed, redeemed, and a child of God.'* You receive in this life what you declare as a child of the living God. As a prudent and obedient child of God, continue to feed on His Word, for in due season, that Word will come forth out of your mouth to silence every voice of the enemy. Amen! As always, the unchanging and powerful Word of God will prevail, to the honor and praise of our God. God's creative power in His Word will begin to bring dead situations back to life and hopeless circumstances to hopeful outcomes, in the mighty name of Jesus Christ. The Word tells us to:

> Trust in the LORD with all your heart, and lean not on your own understanding; in all your ways acknowledge Him, and He shall direct your paths. Do not be wise in your own eyes; fear the LORD and depart from evil. It will be health to your flesh, and strength to your bones. (Proverbs 3:5–8 NKJV).

And remember that, "Heaven and earth will pass away, but My Words will by no means pass away." (Matthew 24:35 NKJV). God's divine Word stands forever, it endures from generation to generation.

Remember the prophet Ezekiel whom God told to prophesy to the dry bones to come alive. The Bible tells us that the hand of the Lord was upon Ezekiel and he was led by the Spirit of God to this valley full of very dry bones of dead people—the Israelites. The Lord asked Ezekiel saying, "Son of man, can these bones live?" In other words, is this situation possible? Is there any hope after that bad report from your doctor? Ezekiel answered, "Sovereign Lord, you alone know." God then told Ezekiel to prophesy to the bones saying to them, "Dry bones, hear the Word of the Lord..." (Ezekiel 37:1–14 NKJV). So, Ezekiel prophesied as he was commanded by the Lord God, and every word he declared came to pass. *When the hand of the Lord is upon your life, when you are led by His Holy Spirit, and you are faithfully living in obedience to His Word, whatever you declare according to His Word shall come to pass. Whatever you ask the Father in the name of Jesus Christ according to His Word and based on His faith in you shall come to pass. The Father not only honors His Word but also honors those that love and trust Him.* Every impossible situation in the sight of man is possible with God only if you believe and work in His Holy Spirit. So, my dear friends, prophesy to those dry bones in your lives saying, "This is what the Word of the sovereign Lord says," in the mighty name of Jesus Christ, you spirit of ... (name whatever you are dealing with) be gone and never to return; I declare... (name what you want to see happen) in the mighty name of Jesus Christ. You must understand the authority under which you operate as a child of God or as children of God; and follow only your blueprint, which is Christ Jesus. The Lord will perfect every Word of His with signs and wonders through His Holy Spirit at work in you, for His glory. My heartfelt prayer is that all people (believers and non-believers) will come to the realization of what Jesus Christ has accomplished for humanity on the cross. May the Holy Spirit of God enlighten the hearts of His people to this revelation that, *Christ is the same yesterday, now, and forever; and what He has said then, He is also saying to us today and forever.* The Word of God remains the same—powerful, unchangeable, and filled with all the fullness of God. Therefore, let us stand on God's Word with all fear and reverence of who He is because there is power in His spoken Word!

4

THE PROMISES OF GOD
ARE YES AND AMEN

God's Word has the power to transform life; His promises will surely come to pass in your life when you are fully committed to the things of God. Through Christ Jesus, all of God's promises in His spoken Word for your life, will certainly be fulfilled, for His glory. Earthly achievements such as fame, power, money, human knowledge, and accomplishment will not bring a person lasting happiness. Humans greatest treasure is their faith in God, in His Word, and its ability to overcome anything on their behalf. All attainment in life is empty, hopeless, and meaningless without God. Our trust should not be in material possessions, which can be taken or faded away, but our trust must be in the Lord Jesus Christ and in His Word. We must fight for what we believe in by obeying what the Word says; our ways must be pleasing in the sight of God. Let the desires of our hearts be in line with God's desire or Word, and He will bring them to pass for His praise and honor. Do not focus on pleasing people but rather let your total attention be on pleasing the Lord, doing that which puts a smile on His face. You cannot worship God and man, or be in the kingdom of this world as well as in the kingdom of God. You must choose what kingdom you want to belong in—God's kingdom or the kingdom of this world? Life is about *choice (God-given choice)*; the Father has given every person the free will to choose. We have the choice to choose light or darkness, good or bad; it is a choice we make each day whether we want to do the things we do or not. If we are for the Lord, then let us be so fully, because only the Lord God deserves all our adoration and praise.

When you know your creator better, you will understand His plan or will for your life better, and hence, serve Him much better. Exercise the muscles of your faith in the Lord and in His Word; persevere in the strengthening of your faith like a muscle because the more you use it, the stronger it becomes. Let us persist to do the will of God, so that we can receive what God has promised (Hebrews 10:36 NIV). Be encouraged by apostle Paul's Words from the Lord:

> Rejoice in the Lord always. I will say it again: Rejoice! Let your gentleness be evident to all. The Lord is near. Do not be anxious about anything, but in every situation, by prayer and petition, with thanksgiving, present your requests to God. And the peace of God, which transcends all understanding, will guard your hearts and your minds in Christ Jesus. (Philippians 4:4–7 NIV).

"And my God will meet all your needs according to the riches of His glory in Christ Jesus." (Philippians 4:19 NIV). God's promises are forever when you are in Christ Jesus and when you abide in Him, in all totality. We must believe in God's Word in entirety for it to come through in our lives; we cannot *'cherry pick' it, do as we like, and when we like.*

And these signs shall follow them that believe; in My name shall they cast out devils; they shall speak with new tongues; they shall take up serpents; and if they drink any deadly thing, it shall not hurt them; they shall lay hands on the sick, and they shall recover. (Mark 16:17–18 KJV).

Stay steadfast in the Lord by remaining in the Word, having the eyes of faith in every Word and allowing the Holy Spirit for His revelation of the Word.

HAVE THE EYES OF FAITH!

Praise the name of the Lord, my friends! I am more excited as we are about to delve into even deeper things in the Lord as the Holy Spirit guides us. May our work in the Lord Jesus continue to be shaped by our faith, our motivation be encouraged by God's love, and our patience be inspired by our hope in the Lord Jesus Christ. And may our understanding of Christ also be enlightened more and more each day, in His mighty name. Amen! We have talked about God's glory including God's intrinsic glory which is the glory that is immeasurable in its magnitude, wisdom, splendor; and God's ascribed glory, which is our gratitude and thankfulness of all that God is, exerted through our prayer, praise, and worship. Our lifestyle of worship, thanksgiving, and praise to God is due to our understanding of His glory and His grace upon us through faith in Him. As we glorify God, we enthrone Him as king of all kings and Lord of lords, and we also overcome and defeat the powers of darkness that surround us and try to influence our walk with the Lord. For us to glorify and reverence God, we must have the *"Eyes of faith!"*

Having the eyes of faith is simply believing, going by, or standing on what the Word of God says. *The Word of God is the evidence to the 'eyes of faith,' whereas our circumstances are the evidence to the natural eyes.* Praise the name of the Lord, we are no more of this natural world and its ways, but we are now born of the Spirit of God! We are in this world, but not of its ways and patterns; we have been translated from the kingdom of darkness into God's marvelous light (into the kingdom of God). The Lord gave Himself for us not only for our sins, but for our total deliverance from this present evil Age. *It is for our total freedom that Christ Jesus has set us free; He has set us free, so that we may live in freedom and no more in bondage of sin and death by the schemes of the enemy.* We are no more a slave to sin and death (spiritual separation from God) but a slave to righteousness, which comes by having the eyes of faith in the Lord Jesus Christ. We, the Gentiles, are a new family of God, a new generation and creation which was promised to Abraham, created through faith in Christ Jesus (righteousness through faith).

You must have the eyes of faith that only see what God sees; see things through the eyes of God—*if God said it, it is final.* When you see what God sees, He is ready to bring it to pass. God is the God that calls things that are not as though they were, He calls the unseen to come forth, and the impossible to feasible, for His pleasure and praise. All things were created out of things that were not seen, but by God's faith in Himself, they all came into being. Likewise, have faith in the promises of God, have faith in every Word God has spoken. Do not allow your present, past, or future circumstances to determine your life, but let the Word of God determine your life. A person is only limited by the Word of God in them and their relationship with the Lord, and not by anything or anyone. Refuse to be moved by what you feel, see, know, or hear; only be moved by what the Word of God says because God's plan is the *only* reality (certainty) for your life. Walking in the plan of God is a lifelong journey of faith, love, joy, and peace, and we must be very intentional. Purposefully declaring positive words based on God's Word will edify, strengthen, heal, restore, and revive you; in other words, the Word of God sustains you and make your way prosperous. Let the words of your mouth and the desires of your heart be in line with the Word of God. Do not waver in doubt, but believe that whatever you declare according to God's Word, has the power to come to pass because of who God is and what He has done. Continue to keep your eyes on the Lord as long as you live; have the eyes of faith, with which you will govern your affairs to live victoriously in the Lord. The Scripture reminds us to "Love the Lord your God with all your heart and with all your soul and with all your mind." (Matthew 22:37 NIV). When you put your trust in the Lord Jesus, in His Word and in His Holy Spirit, He will begin to open the eyes of your understanding (eyes of your heart) to deeper spiritual things, for His glory. Wait patiently in the Word and in faith, my dear friends, do not be despondent but keep your focus on Christ and on Him alone because God always honors His name.

WARFARE AND UNDERSTANDING THE ENEMY

We are constantly living from one warfare to another, from the day we were born to the day we leave this earthly home. For the fact that we are alive, we will go through different trials and challenges (both physical and spiritual). But as children of God, we will go through each warfare in victory because Christ has paid the price and He has overcome the world. Warfare as defined by the Cambridge dictionary is, "The activity of fighting a war or strongly competing, especially with reference to the type of weapons used or the way the fighting is done." There are many wars going on today in the world than you probably know of. It is difficult to grasp the horrible ongoing consequences of these wars, but we must admit that war has become a way of life to millions of people. There is hardly a city in the world where there are no warring conflicts, and it seems to be escalating at an alarming rate. We do not have to be afraid of these battles if our trust is in the Lord Jesus Christ. As Christians, we cannot view the subject of warfare from an interest point of view but from a survival point of view. If we are not prepared to stand against the enemy, we will lose the battle; since it is *a spiritual battle* that we fight, and it must be a way of life. The enemy is ruthless in his attack against God's children, but thank God we can declare the Word and enjoy our victory through Jesus Christ.

The purpose of warfare is mainly for power and control over something or someone else by using force. Thus, the spirit behind warfare is *'greed or covetousness;'* a covetous or greedy person is driven by continual dissatisfaction; such a person is never content with what he or she has. He forms images in his mind of having and controlling what others have. That person may be religious and attempts to justify his actions as being righteous and in the interest of others. Lucifer (Satan) for example, according to the Bible (Genesis 1; Luke 10; Revelation 9 NKJV), went a step further and believed he could replace God. He coveted what God had and attempted to seize power through praise. Satan wanted to control every angelic being in heaven and be worshipped as God was. As a result, one third of the angels followed this self-exalted god. But Satan's power was and is insignificant, compared to God's power and glory; and in the end, Satan was cast out of heaven with the other rebellious angels. Before we can begin to understand the significance of warfare, we need to know its origin. There was a time when there was no war, but only peace. *Peace as we know is not the nonexistence of war, but the power and friendship (companionship) of God. When we are justified through our faith in Christ, we have peace (power and companionship) with the Father through His Son.* When God created angels and humanity, His intension was for them to love and serve Him. But due to sin (disobedience), Lucifer took his eyes off God and placed them on himself. His desires became greater and more important than fulfilling the desire of the one who created, anointed, and loved him. Sin was born when Lucifer stopped giving worship to God and started to see his own worth as being greater than that of

God. He began to idolize himself through vain imaginations and demanded worship that he felt he was worthy of. One third of the angels worshipped and followed him, and his cravings for worship has never ceased. The cross of calvary delivered the death blow, and he now knows he is defeated. However, Lucifer will continue with a fanatical, insatiable desire to be in control of the lives of people. When he is in control, he is a god to those he controls, and in a cheap distorted way, receives worship from them. The unsaved or a person living in total unbelief of the Lord Jesus Christ has placed a high esteem on himself and everything else, rather than on God, their creator. This self-gratification perpetuates the spirit of the devil and enmity with God.

We need to be aware that in as much as there is warfare in the natural realm, there is also warfare in the spiritual realm. In the natural realm, the desire to control another person is done through the occupation of land, using force, and violence; and the general rule is that if one occupies the land, he controls the people. But please be aware that warfare has a spiritual root, and we can translate this into spiritual warfare. We see exactly that the same principles apply in spiritual warfare as in natural warfare. There is a war between the kingdom of darkness and the kingdom of light. The kingdom of darkness wants to occupy the inheritance that God has secured for those that love Him through our Lord and savior Jesus Christ. Our godly inheritance is here for us to occupy by faith in Christ, but the devil will attack with any weapon that he can use to nullify the effectiveness of Christ's victory in us. Nevertheless, God will continue to build His church or kingdom through a people who believe and receive the covenant of inheritance He has provided in Christ Jesus. *It is important for us to grasp the fact that Satan has limited power in the realm of the spiritual world. He is not omniscient, omnipresent, or omnipotent and neither are his angels. But we serve a God who is omniscient, omnipresent, and omnipotent.* Also, be aware of the warnings the Word of God gives us that, there is more demonic influence and activity today than ever before. False prophets and teachers that follow deceiving spirits and demons will be found even in the body of Christ (1 Timothy 4:1 NIV). If Christ had a Judas among His twelve disciples, you could imagine how the church will be infiltrated with darkness in these End Times. We must be enlightened and prepared or we will never stand against this spiritual warfare. It truly is a spiritual battle and therefore, we must be sober in spirit, alert, and vigilant against the spiritual forces of darkness that are looking for opportunities to devour God's children (1 Peter 5:8 NIV). Do not believe or put your faith in every spirit but discerned, tested, resisted, and rejected every spirit through the power in the Word, the name of Jesus, and the Spirit of God (1 John 4:1–6 NIV). As children of God, He expects us not only to be aware of their existence, but to overcome them in the mighty name of Jesus Christ through the power of the Holy Spirit.

The devil has so many ways of attacking God's children. For example, when we place human interests before godly ones, we place ourselves in danger of being demonically influenced. Our dealing with money for instance, is a target for Satan to gain entrance and influence us. But our personal knowledge of God's Word is our deliverance from demonic influences. The Bible encourages us to put on God's armor in Ephesians saying:

> Finally, my brethren, be strong in the Lord and in the power of His might. Put on the whole armor of God, that you may be able to stand against the wiles of the devil. For we do not wrestle against flesh and blood, but against principalities, against powers, against the rulers of the darkness of this age, against spiritual hosts of wickedness in the heavenly places. Therefore, take up the whole armor of God, that you may be able to withstand in the evil day, and having done all, to stand. Stand therefore, having girded your

waist with truth, having put on the breastplate of righteousness, and having shod your feet with the preparation of the gospel of peace; above all, taking the shield of faith with which, you will be able to quench all the fiery darts of the wicked one. And take the helmet of salvation, and the sword of the Spirit, which is the Word of God, praying always with all prayer and supplication in the Spirit, being watchful to this end with all perseverance and supplication for all the saints. (Ephesians 6:10–18 NKJV).

Stand on the Word, my dear friends, and do not be dismayed or moved, for signs and wonders follow the Word of God!

SIGNS AND WONDERS SHALL ACCOMPANY THOSE WHO BELIEVE

Whether you have a relationship with the Father or not, whether you know Him personally or not; it does not change the fact that God has beautifully and perfectly created you for a *specific purpose* here on earth. The master has need of you, and that is why you are never a mistake or here on this earth by chance; you were born for God's glory and for a specific task that only you could fulfill. However, this purpose will only come to fulfillment when are in tune or in line with your creator, when you surrender to the Lord Jesus Christ as your personal savior. Once you are edified in the knowledge of Christ, you also discover God's will for your life through the help of His Holy Spirit in you. The Holy Spirit is the one that approves our salvation, and without Him we can do nothing in the Lord. *Without the relationship and fellowship with the Holy Spirit, our Christian life will only be but a dead religion with no power or presence of God.* There is no true church without the Holy Spirit. We will talk more on the importance of the person of the Holy Spirit later. When we examine the Scriptures, from the Old Testament times to the New Testament, we may wonder why God performed so many miraculous signs and wonders among His people. Even during Christ's time on earth, as well as during the time of His apostles, signs and wonders accompanied them everywhere as the Lord worked with them through the power of the Holy Spirit (Mark 16:20 NKJV). These miraculous signs and wonders performed by the Holy Spirit were written in the Scriptures to declare God's sovereignty and power over all things. Also, the Holy Spirit performs astonishing signs and wonders so that people may believe that our Lord Jesus is the Christ (the anointed one), the Son of God, and that by believing (trusting, cleaving to, and relying on Him) we may have life in His name (John 20: 31 NIV). If you have made the Lord Jesus your personal savior, believe also in His Word, and be led by His Spirit without a shadow of doubt. Hence, signs and wonders shall surely follow those that believe in Him.

Believing and abiding in Christ Jesus is a vital key to signs and wonders. Believing in what Christ Jesus did on the cross, the power in His name, and believing in our inheritance in Him as children of God, bring forth abiding fruits in us. When the Lord calls you and sets before you a specific work for His glory, you must surrender and believe in every aspect of His Word pertaining to His calling. Then the Holy Spirit will lead and guide you, work with you, and confirm His Word through supernatural miracles. Christ Jesus, on His way to heaven, gave His disciples the great commission:

> Go into all the world and preach the gospel to all creation. Whoever believes and is baptized will be saved, but whoever does not believe will be condemned. And these signs will accompany those that believe: In My name they will drive out demons; they will speak in new tongues; they

will pick up snakes with their hands; and when they drink deadly poison, it will not hurt them at all; they will place their hands on sick people, and they will get well. (Mark 16:15–18 NIV).

Paul, Barnabas, and the other apostles were all led by the Holy Spirit, who confirmed His Word by great signs and wonders. That same commission is also true for us today, for those He has called to His service and for His glory. If the Lord has assigned you to a specific task or work, He will glorify and honor His name and honor you in every way. No schemes of the devil will prevail in God's work nor in your life.

The Word tells us that, "Jesus Christ is the same yesterday, today and forever" (Hebrews 13:8 NIV); what He has done before, He can still do today, and forever. The same Holy Spirit that was at work in the prophets of old, the same Spirit acted during Christ Jesus' ministry, and the same one that raised Him from the dead, is the same Spirit that descended upon the disciples on the day of Pentecost. That same Spirit is still with us on earth today; and He is in us as the seal confirming that we are children of God through our faith in Christ Jesus. Remember, that in this life we are like Christ Jesus (1 John 4:17 NIV), and greater things shall we do in His name because we believe and abide in Him. Christ Jesus is our source of life, and without Him we are nothing, and can do absolutely nothing that will endure. We must be connected in Him, and in His Word, and the Holy Spirit must be alive and at Work in us, to attain our full God-given potential. So, as you go about your daily schedule, just remember that you were created for the mighty, to do great things in the Lord. Never forget that, "Everything is possible for the one that believes." (Mark 9:23 NIV). Only believe in the Lord, as God is faithful to His Word!

GOD'S FAITHFULNESS IS ALL AROUND US

Father, in the name of our Lord Jesus Christ, may You be exalted in our nation, and in all nations of the world. May You be exalted in our lives, in our families, in our homes, in our circumstances, in our jobs, in our relationships, in our children, in our finances, in our businesses, and above all, be exalted in our work with You O God. May all Your creation praise You, and Your saints adore You; and may Your knowledge through Christ Jesus fill the hearts and minds of Your people all over the world, even as the waters cover the seas. In Your mighty and glorious name, Lord Jesus. Amen!

The Holy Spirit gave me the above prayer during fellowship with the Lord, and I knew He wanted me to share it with His people. At the end of our fellowship, the Lord also gave me this word that, "His faithfulness is all around us." As a result, the Lord must be exalted in all areas of our lives. Talk about the goodness, the power, the greatness, the holiness, the faithfulness, and the character of God through His Son Jesus Christ in every area of your life. Then the enemy will have no place in your heart because all your thoughts, imaginations, and acts will be consumed by the Word of God. The Spirit of God is moving all over the world, and all around us, regardless of the turmoil going on in the world. God is still at work, and His divine will and purpose for His creation still prevail, because His faithfulness is all around us. What God has destined for you, will surely come to pass as you dwell in Him; and no devil in hell will be able to stop it. The Lord will build you and you shall be built; He will perfect every imperfection in you for His name's sake. Do not look at any present situation my friends; the master who is the creator of all things is at work in you and will bring you to an expected end for His glory. Every morning, He wakes you up on time, with a sound mind, and in strength for another day; anything could have happened to you while sleeping, but God's grace kept you yet another day. The Lord takes you out safely in His favor and brings you back in one piece; yes, this is another of the Father's faithfulness that is all around you. God's breath of life in you, His favor, His mercy, and grace are more examples of His unfailing faithfulness. The sun, moon, the vast universe, night, day, seasons, air, rain, living, and non-living things, all declare the glory and majesty of His loving-kindness poured upon us each moment of our lives. If we were to list all of God's faithfulness towards His creation, it would take all of eternity. But in everything, we must show our gratitude to God through thanksgiving, prayer, and praise.

There is no excuse for not giving God all the glory that is due Him, since everything the Lord has done and created exemplify His existence, glory, awesomeness, loving-kindness, faithfulness, greatness, and power. For you to be alive even this very moment is a miracle and a gift of God, otherwise you will be consumed by the enemy the devil. So, wherever you find yourself and in whatever you do, may the name of the Lord Jesus be exalted above every other name. And at the mention of the name of Christ Jesus, may every situation in your life bow, may every chain be broken, and every shut door in your life be opened in the mighty name of Jesus Christ. Amen, because Christ Jesus is now seated at the right hand of the Father, interceding for us. All power in heaven and on earth belongs to Christ because of His obedience, and He has given to us that same power in His name. There is everlasting power in you and at work in you at the mention of the name of Jesus Christ through His Spirit in you. *Live in this reality—that, there is power in the Word of God, the name of Jesus Christ, and His Holy Spirit; live by His faith.*

THE JUST SHALL LIVE BY FAITH

The Holy Spirit wants to remind us once more about the importance of faith in the believer's life and work with the Lord.

The righteous, as we may be aware, are all those people who believe in the sacrificial atonement of Christ Jesus for our sins, those that have right standing with God through faith in Him, and faith in His Word. Those who do not only believe but also walk or live according to what they have believed (the Word of God). Believe is action; our actions and ways of life evidence what we believe in our hearts. *Christ Jesus is our righteousness revealed in the gospel; the righteousness that is no more based on 'works but a righteousness that comes through faith in the entirety of God including His salvation (Christ Jesus)—His birth, life, death, resurrection, and second coming.* This mystery of God, that was hidden for years throughout the generations, that was spoken about throughout the entire Scriptures, has now been made known to us through Christ Jesus in the flesh. Our faith in Christ has now qualified us righteous and justified before God our Father.

When we talk about faith, we are looking at a *living thing,* with all the characteristics of a living thing. Just like the air we breathe that we cannot see but it most certainly exists, real, and powerful. Likewise, faith is a living substance in every individual the Lord has created; we cannot physically see faith but is *real, alive,* and *active* when activated in the believer. Faith is so powerful that it can move mountains (the impossible); it can move any mountain in your life through its wonder working power. Faith is so fundamental that without it, according to the Word, it is impossible to walk and even please God, as faith is the foundation of our relationship with the Father through the Son. We cannot have a relationship with God nor please Him or even exist without faith. That is why we must learn from faith and fight for it; we cannot afford not to activate our faith, or we will lose it, since our existence is dependent upon our faith in the Lord Jesus Christ. Faith is the believer's power, weapon, foundation, and source of everything; our entire survival and source of life is based on our faith. But "What is faith?" *Faith is believing that God exists, believing in His glory, power, and salvation; faith is believing that god is gracious to those that love Him and seek after Him. In other words, faith is 'totally believing' in who God is, His Word, and what He has done; it is 'not trying to figure out God' but 'accepting' what has been freely done for us.* As a believer, you must live and operate under the authority of the name of Jesus Christ. God exalted Christ Jesus to the highest place because of His humility and obedience. Our absolute belief in God's authority will bring to pass whatever we desire and declare according to His Word.

The Word tells us that, "The just shall live by faith." (Romans 1:17 NKJV). Those that are justified through faith in Christ must live in that faith; we must live by the Word of God, without questioning, or trying to figure it out. Your faith will bring the future into the present without a shadow of doubt. For example, "I am healed;" see yourself healed; see that new job; see that new home; see that breakthrough in your family, breakthrough in your finances, and in all areas of your life. Let the faith of Christ in your heart comes forth in the words you declare. Speak life changing Word of God to that situation in your life in the mighty name of Jesus Christ, and see the power in His name bring those things you have asked for in prayer into existence. When you live by faith in God's Word, your entire being will be filled with His Spirit, leaving no room in your soul to indulge in the sinful desires of the flesh. Your faith in Christ, in His Word and salvation, is the way to the kingdom of God, and the key that unlocks every door in your life. Our faith is not based on what is seen in the physical, nor is it based on how we feel, our present situations or our know-how; but our faith is built on Christ Jesus and Him alone. Christ said, "Therefore I tell you, whatever you ask for in prayer, believe that you have received it, and it will be yours." (Mark 11:24 NIV). Believing is the key—your faith! Remember the woman with the issue of blood (blood disease); none of the members of her body could make her healed, but her faith. She believed in her heart that if she could only touch the hem of Christ's garment, she would be healed. She put her faith into action, after hearing the good news of the gospel. And indeed, she was healed when she moved in that belief, with her eyes on the Lord her healer. This woman did not just sit down and complain, she fought her way through the crowd, most probably been pushed and shoved about. But she held on, with her eyes on the price (her healing and life again). Glory to God! We must fight for our faith (a good fight of faith), and never let go no matter what the situation may be. God can do exceedingly, above all that we could ever ask, think, or even imagine; He is faithful to whatsoever He has promised! His peace that surpasses all human knowledge and understanding is ours because of our justification through faith in Him.

We all live by faith daily because faith is applied in every area of our lives. For instance, we believe that when we go to bed at night, we will wake up in the morning, that we will make it safely to work or home; we even believe that our tomorrow would be better. The same way you have faith in your everyday routine, the same way it should be applied in your spiritual work and relationship with the Father through Christ. Begin to see what God sees and allow His Word to come alive through your faith in the power of His Holy Spirit. Your faith is vital as a child of God; thus, it must be very intentional, directed, exercised, and disciplined. It is not the faith of your brother, sister, father, mother, or your pastor, but yours—your faith. Christ Jesus is the origin of our faith and He is the one that perfects us through the power of His Holy Spirit in us. Declare life into that lifeless situation (fear, anxiety, worthlessness, disappointment, pain, sickness, unforgiveness, and worry) in the mighty name of Jesus. The name of Jesus Christ is still effectual as always, and forever it will be. Take the name of Jesus with you wherever you go and hold fast to it, come what may, because His promises are sure!

GOD'S PROMISES

The Lord's faithfulness to all His creation and to His Word, is one aspect of God's character that overwhelms me time and time again. God is not just a just God, but He is also true to His own nature and promises. Being the alpha and omega, the beginning and the end of all things in heaven and on earth, the creator of everything, visible, and invisible; God is above all principalities, powers, rulers, and dominion, and there is no end to His kingdom. Everything will pass away, but His Word stands firm forever; it is eternal and will surely come to pass because He is faithful to every Word He has spoken—*nothing or no one can put a stop to God's Word*. The faith of Christ Jesus in you will bring to pass the Word of God you declare. God is His Word, and His Word is truthful, right, and faithful in every way; He cannot deny Himself. The Word of God is the power and source of life—the force, which holds all things together. We must trust all of God's Word and His promises, and not just believe in a chosen few. Whatever the Word says concerning your life or any situation, that is what you should follow. If He says He is the God that heals you, then say 'Amen' to it, stand on that Word, trusting in the Lord. All you must do is surrender to His will for your life and allow His blood to cleanse you from all unrighteousness. We serve a faithful God, and what He has said before in the Scriptures, are still applicable to us today. His Word is the same for every season in our lives, and will surely come to pass only if we believe in Him with every fiber of our being.

When you totally trust in the Lord, you become dead to yourself and dead to the fleshy desires of this world. As apostle Paul stated, "I have been crucified with Christ and I no longer live, but Christ lives in me. The life I now live in the body, I live by faith in the Son of God, who loved me and gave Himself for me." (Galatians 2:20 NIV). It is no longer you that lives, but Christ Jesus that lives in you through faith in Him. You no longer rely on your strength, wisdom, nor human ideologies of this world but you totally trust in Him who has loved you and died for you. Your mind, thoughts, and actions become more like Christ, full of the knowledge and wisdom of Christ Jesus through the power of the Holy Spirit. God's Word is our blueprint and path to follow; the Spirit of God in us is alive and active and changes us each day as we live and abide in His Word. God's living Word in us brings forth light within our soul because when God's light enters and takes root in a heart, it brings life (eternal life) into that soul, making that person a new creation or born again in their mind. As you spend time in the Word, your mind begins to renew to that of the Lord's through the help of His Spirit in you. Hence, it is no more the old you that lives, but Christ now lives in you through His Spirit; and the fear of God in you now surpasses the fear of man and that of this world.

As stated earlier, God's Word is life and has the power to restore and give life to hopeless circumstances because God is the God of impossibilities. For instance, when the doctors say there is no hope, that is when God says there is hope. Put your hope and trust in the Lord, in His saving grace, which is in Christ Jesus. Do not put your trust in people, or in things of this temporary world; but put your faith in God's unchanging eternal Word. Feed your spirit daily with His Word to the point of total immersion in Him; to the point that the fruit of the Holy Spirit is manifested in every area of your life. When people see you, may they see the glory and love of the Father all around you and through you; may His Word come alive in you and change your walk with Him forever, in Jesus' mighty name. Amen! Whatever God has said in His Word, is done already! Be rest assured when you declare God's Word because His Word is settled (already established) in heaven. *It has nothing to do with you, but it has all to do with Him; it is not about you, not about your reputation, but all about Jesus Christ and Him alone!* Rest in Him, my dear friends!

EVERYTHING IS WELL IN CHRIST

Have you ever wondered why God would give us a task knowing that in our own physical strength we will never be able to achieve it? The reason is that God longs for our constant *intimacy and fellowship* with Him. The Lord Jesus wants us to totally depend on Him for His leadership and guidance through His Spirit. He tells us that, if we live in Him and He in us through His Word and fellowship, we will bear much fruit; and apart from Him the result is an unfulfilled life. We must remain in Christ, and His Word must take pre-eminence in our lives through faith. *This means an on-going true relationship with the Lord Jesus and not a religious practice at certain times of the week, month, or year. It is not a relationship only on Sunday mornings or Wednesday evenings, but an eternal and true relationship based on the Word of God and led by His Holy Spirit.* God wants us to totally trust in Him with our entire being and to depend not on our own ways and understanding.

The Lord Jesus wants to lead and guide you one step at a time, so that you will depend on His guidance and develop an intimate relationship with Him, starting right here on earth. If you could do His given task in your own power and strength, then you will take the glory. But when you rely wholly on God even for your next breath, then He takes the glory. Even though the journey might seem too hard, you must remember that you are *following the leader of the pack (the Holy Spirit)*; He controls the movement and path of His people. Christ is certainly the good shepherd, who loves His flock so much to the point of laying down His own life for them. God wants His children to know who they are in Him, to know their rights in Him, follow His example, and have His mindset. When God told Abraham to leave his Father's house, he simply obeyed as he was led by his faith in God. Likewise, my dear friend, have hope in the assignment the Lord has given you; it will lead to the development of your faith in the Lord Jesus. Whatever instruction or vision the Lord has laid in your heart, there is a set provision for it to be manifested in the physical. In Christ, everything is going to be alright; the Lord will perfect everything concerning you. God has blessed us in Christ Jesus with all spiritual blessings in heavenly realms (Ephesians 1:3 NIV), but we must rely on Him as our loving Father. In Christ Jesus, God will work all things out for the good of those that love Him and are called according to His purpose (Romans 8:28 NIV). In Christ, we can do all things, because His Spirit empowers us through each challenge along the way. He supplies our *every* need; not *some* of our needs, but *every* need! That includes our pains, our sicknesses, our finances, our marriage, our faith, and our weaknesses; Christ is our *all* and in *all*!

FAITH—THE ONLY FIGHT

Let us talk a little bit more about the concept of faith, because it is the fundamental tool upon which everything was built, is built, and will be built. Faith is so important that we need to fight for it; it is the only fight that we (humans) need to fight. Faith originates from God the Father, who is the creator and Lord of all. For God's people to establish a true relationship with Him, they must start with faith. Without faith, there is no true spiritual relationship with God because God is a Spirit, and He must be worshiped in the Spirit through faith in His Word. As we stated earlier, faith is a vital aspect and the 'centerpiece' of our relationship with God. Faith is a gift from God just like the other gifts of God such as salvation, prophesy, healing, and so on and so forth. *Faith is a gift to the believer in God and in His Word; the very first thing that we need to activate in order to start a relationship with the Father or even please Him.* "And without faith, it is impossible to please God, because anyone who comes to Him must believe that He exists and that He rewards those who earnestly seek Him." (Hebrews 11:6 NIV). It is only by faith that one can understand the things of God through the help of the Holy Spirit. Faith is applied in every area of our lives—from the time you wake up to the time you go to bed. It is faith that makes you believe that when you go to bed at night, you will wake up in the morning, or when you get into your car, bus, or train that you will make it safely to your destination. Faith gives you hope for the future and it is what makes your life worth living. The same way you have faith in your daily routine, the same way it should be applied in your relationship with the Father. Understanding this concept of faith is life changing in the knowledge, worship, relationship, and understanding of Christ Jesus. Come now, let us walk by faith!

WHAT IS FAITH?

We talked about faith, the only fight we need to fight, and that it is applied in all areas of life and godliness. But what is *faith*? Let us briefly state it again that, faith is a gift from God and alive; it is also a living thing with all the attributes of a living thing. According to the Word of God, "Faith is the substance of things hoped for, the evidence of things not seen." (Hebrews 11:1 NKJV). One aspect of faith is *'totally believing'* in God (His acts and salvation); it is knowing and understanding who God is in all totality leading to reverential fear of Him. *Faith is not trying to believe but accepting* what has been freely done for us; it is having the confidence that God's Word will surely come to pass because of what Christ Jesus did on the cross. Faith brings the future into the present without a shadow of doubt. Faith is seeing what God sees for your life; having God's vision, and our Father, who is faithful to His Word, will bring it to pass. Do not look at your situation, but see the solution based on the Word of God. One's faith is developed by hearing the Word, spending time in the Word, and through fellowship in prayer. After being certain of what is heard and read, faith comes through the power of the Holy Spirit of God, and that Word of God planted in your soul begins to germinate and convicts the heart. This continuous growth in your faith in Christ Jesus leads to a lasting relationship with Him. Abraham, our Father of Faith, believed in God without wavering, and it was accredited to him as righteousness. Righteousness is not as a result of works or good deeds, rather righteousness is of faith in Christ Jesus—*believing* in God's Word. So, let the faith in your heart be evidenced in the words of your mouth, in your actions, and let it be in line with God's Word.

FAITH NOT KNOWING

When I think of faith, I perceive it as, *'faith not knowing'* because it reflects on our entire journey of life with the Lord Jesus, especially when He called our family to move from London, United Kingdom to the United States. The Lord clearly revealed to my family through a vision that He has a need for our family and that we must be dead to ourselves—meaning that we must be dead to our desires and aspirations of this world, and totally surrender to His will. This was the hardest decision we have ever made as a family of seven, leaving the known for the unknown. Like our father of faith, Abraham, we had no option but to obey the voice of the Lord our God, and He has *never* failed us, *not once!* It is our faith in God and our willingness in obedience that moves Him, and not our excellence of words, nor our knowledge, or status. With obedience comes the supernatural flow of God's blessings; the impossible things become possible, and miracles begin to happen as we yield to the will of God. Our faith in God is the key to the heart of the Father; it is not based on what is seen in the physical, how we feel, or our present situation but it is built on Christ Jesus and Him alone. Let us bring the spiritual into the physical without wavering in unbelief of our hearts; let us fill our minds with the powerful Word of God as we stand on every Word the Father has spoken, been confident that He will do whatsoever He has promised.

LET US LIVE BY FAITH

Now that we know the truth about faith in the Lord, we must live by it. Our actions should reflect our knowledge of Christ Jesus and our faith in Him. "As the body without the spirit is dead, so faith without deeds is dead." (James 2:26 NIV). Another aspect of faith is *action*; you act based on your belief; you cannot say I believe in Christ Jesus or I am a Christian if your actions are contrary to that of Christ or His Word. Your lifestyle and relationship with the Lord and with others should show forth your faith. Your mindset must reflect that of the Father as a child of God through your faith in Him. For example, you cannot say you love God if you cannot love your fellow human. God is love and anyone who loves is born of God and knows God; He or she that does not love, does not know God or love Him. Your actions of faith will overcome any circumstance you face because Christ Jesus has overcome the world through His atoning sacrifice on the cross and His resurrection. He reminds us that, He is the way, the truth and the life; that no one will go the Father except through Him (John 14:6 NIV).

Christ Jesus is the truth that comes from the Father unto us through faith in Him; and this truth will set us free from the devil's snares. Remember, we are no longer a slave to sin but a slave to righteousness through faith in the Lord Jesus. But if you know the truth and you still choose not to live by faith in the truth, then you are living in sin and disobedience, which will lead to God's discipline and wrath. God is very patient and loving, and it grieves His Heart to have to discipline His children or see them perish due to disobedience. Though God may have to rebuke sin and disobedience in the lives of His children, His love for humanity remains forever and He will never abandon us. Do not forsake what you know, you must live by faith in Christ as a child of God.

The ancients or those of faith before us were commended for their unshakeable faith in God's spoken Word; all the prophets of God believed in God, His Word and His acts—their entire lifestyle was that of faith. Since faith is also action; we believe, and we act upon that belief according to God's Word. For instance, God is love, therefore, you love others as a child of God, and your actions reflect that love of God in you. You forgive because you believe that Christ has forgiven your own sins when you confessed them; you obey God's Word because you love Him. Your faith in Christ Jesus will affect every action and overcome every scheme of the devil. Nothing in this world is worth more than your faith in the Lord Jesus, as everything will pass away like a fleeting shadow, but His Word will *never* pass away. Hence, hold on to what you have believed to the very end, so that no one takes your crown. Let us be encouraged by the Words of apostle Paul saying, "Being confident of this, that He who has began a good work in you will bring it to completion until the day of Christ Jesus." (Philippians 1:6 NIV).

FAITH LIKE A MUSTARD SEED

Faith brings forth the impossibility to possibility; it brings to pass God's promises after building total confidence in God and in His Word. This faith is not from human nature but from Christ Jesus—it is a gift. Human faith was not enough then and is certainly not enough even now. We must have the living faith of God, which is the faith of Christ Jesus our Lord. If you do not have faith, simply ask the Lord Jesus for the gift of faith to believe in Him, in His Spirit and in His Word. We can only win the battles of this life through our faith in the Word and in the name of Jesus Christ our Lord. But we know that Satan the devil always tries to destroy what God has done. He corrupts the minds and hearts of people so that they do not believe the truth of God or worship the Father. As stated before, Satan's aim from the beginning has being to receive worship like God; and he goes all out to turn the hearts of people from giving God the worship, through unbelief and deviating from the truth, which is the Word of God. Satan knows that when God's people know the truth, the truth will set them free—free from every bondage he has instilled upon them. So, my dear friends in the Lord, stand on the truth of God's Word and allow it to dwell in you and through you, in the power of His Holy Spirit. And no weapons forged against you from any agent of the devil shall prevail if you remain in the Lord Jesus and trust in His Word.

FULLY TRUST THE LORD JESUS

When you trust someone, you are rest assured that they have your back in all situations; like a true friend, who is always there. But the Word of God tells us that, "There is a friend that sticks closer than a brother." (Proverbs 18:24 NIV). Trusting in the Lord Jesus is the right way to go, because your faith in God leads to your total trust in His unfailing love and faithfulness. When you fully trust in the Lord Jesus, you become dead to yourself, dead to your own ways. You do not rely on your own understanding anymore but fully rely on the Lord's—*fear of the 'what ifs' and 'but' disappear.* As a child of God, you are no longer anxious about anything because you are fully persuaded of whom you have believed and you are convinced of who you are in Christ, and certain of your inheritance in Him. As you walk with the Lord, your trust, faith, hope, and love grow from glory to glory in Him and with others around you. The Word of God becomes alive in your life and the Lord in return begins to trust you with deeper things of God. This relationship with the Lord Jesus will get to a level of total trust and love, whereby, He will act on our behalf even before we ask. This act of God was cited by the prophet Isaiah, "Before they call, I will answer; while they are still speaking, I will hear." (Isaiah 65:24 NIV). *Wow,* what a mighty and faithful God we serve!

GOD WATCHES OVER HIS OWN

Remember that as a child of God, you belong to Him, and He watches over you, His own. When you make the Lord Jesus your Lord over all areas of your life, He then becomes the boss of your life. He keeps His righteous right hand of protection and seal over you. So, whatsoever you ask the Father in the name of Jesus Christ (while believing in your heart), you shall receive. If God's eyes are on the sparrow and all the other creatures, what about you whom He created in His image and likeness, whom He suffered and died for on the cross, and rose again for your justification. Yes, the Lord loves you with unconditional and everlasting love and He will also watch over every affair of your life if you lay it at His feet in faith. The question is, do you love the Lord and are you willing to surrender at His feet?' Those who trust in the Lord Jesus will never be put to shame (1 Peter 2:6 NIV). No matter the circumstance, just surrender to the Lord Jesus, because He cares for you. Commit all your ways to the Lord in faith, even as you delight in Him, and He will bring them to pass for His glory and pleasure. He will strengthen every weakness because He is our strength and perfect all our imperfections, for His name's sake.

Again, I say according to the Word of God, "Trust in the Lord with all your heart and lean not on your own understanding; in all your ways acknowledge Him, and He shall direct your paths." (Proverbs 3:5–6 NKJV). All of God's promises are 'yes and amen' and will surely come to pass. Every spoken or written Word of the Father is true; it has already come to pass, that is why it is written. God's Word endures forever and ever in heaven, on earth, and in all of creation. Always, see through God's eyes (through faith) and declare what His Word says because there is power in the spoken Word of God!

5

GOD'S WORD IS HIS WILL

The Word of God is the *"Will"* of God, the Father, for His children. The first and fundamental will of God for our lives is eternal life. This eternal life, according to our Lord Jesus Christ, comes *by knowing the Father, the only true God, and Jesus Christ, whom He has sent* (John 17:3 NIV). God's divine will for all people is to be saved and come to the knowledge of the truth, namely Christ Jesus and His Word (1 Timothy 2:4 NIV). God wants His people to first get to know Him and have an everlasting relationship with Him; and then all other things (including our aspirations of this world that we tend to worry about) shall be added freely unto us. You may wonder why the God of the universe would desire an everlasting relationship with mere mortal like us. God is love and He made us in His love and desires that we live eternally with Him in love. But humans' continual sinful nature separates them from God; from having a loving and trusting relationship with their maker. This spiritual separation is because God is holy, and in Him there is no darkness at all; thus, His people must be holy and blameless before His presence. Believing in His salvation for sin makes us righteous and holy before His presence, giving us eternal life in Him.

Being obedient to the will of God is the true bread that satisfies the human soul. Feed on this life-giving bread and live a fulfilled life here on earth and into eternity; feed on God's Word so that you can grow spiritually and be the man or woman that you were created to be. Let your thoughts plus your actions be in line with the Word of God, and God, in His infinite faithfulness, will bring every Word of His to pass. Remember God's Word is His will for His children, and this does not change, it has not changed, and it will never change; you determine and choose whether you want to receive from God or not. Yes, God has given us the free will or choice; we are the determining factor for receiving from God. We choose either to be in the kingdom of this fleeting world or God's everlasting kingdom; we either choose death or life.

God's Word is His will because there is supernatural power in His Word. The Bible is God's Word available to us; it is the plan of life for those that believe in Christ Jesus (the giver of life), for those that love Him, and trust in Him. It is the Father's will that we do not conform to the pattern of this world once we become born of His Spirit, but rather be transformed to the image of His Son by the renewing of our minds through the power of His Spirit and His Word. As a new creation in Christ, let us desire more of Him day in and day out, until we are filled to a point of outpouring His Word. Believers in Christ need to understand the inheritance and authority that they have in Jesus Christ—what He has freely given unto us, the depth of His love for us, and what He has prepared for those that love and trust in Him. Christ has already paid for *all* that you and I would ever need, and *all* the answers are in His Word. He is the answer to every problem, the solution to every challenge because He has paid the price, and the victory is won! Glory to God! If you need healing for your body, He is the healer; if you do not know which way to go, He is the way; Christ is all that we need. We need to abide totally in Him and in His Word, and the power of His Holy Spirit will bring to pass every spoken Word of God. God and His Word are inseparable because He is His Word—powerful, faithful, and true! The Word in Ephesians tells us, "Now to Him who is able to do immeasurably more than all we ask or imagine, according to His power that is at work within us, to Him be glory in the church and in Christ Jesus throughout all generations, forever and ever! Amen." (Ephesians 3:20 NIV). God's spoken Word will never fail; it is the truth, and it stands forever and ever. *The Word of God does not put a person in bondage but sets free those that trust in His name; the name (Jesus Christ) that is above every other name.* Whatever situation you may be going through, if it has a name, then the name of Jesus Christ surpasses that name; so, declare the name of Jesus according to His Word in that situation. Every Word of God is His will, and He is more than able to bring to pass *all* that He has promised.

God's Word is the key to our entire existence; we cannot survive successfully in this life without the Word of God—in us and at work in us, through His Holy Spirit. Living in the Word is *true success* in the sight of God. True success is doing that which is pleasing in the sight of God; living a life that reflects the image and likeness of their creator and giving glory to Him. As stated before, God's Word is the plan that He wants His children (born of His Spirit) to follow. Let us start this relationship with the Lord Jesus by keeping His Word in our mouth always (declaring His Word always) which will lead to our love for the Word of God. This love of God in our hearts will compel us to hunger and thirst for righteousness day in and day out through the power of the Holy spirit in us. Feeding your spirit with the Word of God will bring you to an expected end—abundant life in the Lord. Similarly, if you do not feed your spirit with the Word of God according to the Spirit of God, your spirit will starve and eventually die. This results to lack of interest in anything to do with God, which is spiritual death or separation from the presence of God. When this spiritual separation happens, a person is no longer under God's shelter, leaving them exposed to the kingdom of darkness to take control of their entire being. *When your love for*

God, for His Word, and for others begin to go cold, know that your spirit is thirsty and hungry for the living Word of God; feed your spirit to prevent spiritual separation from God. Remember that what you put in your body, spirit, and soul, is what comes out; the things you watch, listen to, read, hear, talk about, and interact with, are the things that will come out of you. If you talk negative things, it indicates the things you feed your soul and spirit with. As children of God, we must study the worthy things of God, we must feed on His Word, in order to edify and strengthen our faith and relationship with the Lord and others around us.

The Word has power to set the captives free and power to make our way prosperous in the Lord. God's Word is His divine will for every aspect of life. There is power in words, so declare what the Word of God says because the words you speak are the bridge between the spiritual world and the physical world. God's Word is Spirit and life and can create; it can change impossible situation to possibility. It is only through the Word of God that we can overcome any situation, only through the Word that we can have life, prosperous life in Christ. Hence, do not agree with the enemy by declaring negative things in your life but profess what you want to see happen, according to the Word of God. *Christ used the Word, and He overcame the world and the devil; we must also speak what God says, speak the Word, see victory, and embrace it.*

Saying what you have (talking about the problem) has no power to change the situation you are in. Stop talking or complaining about the problem; instead, speak what God speaks concerning the problem—in His Word. *Whatever you allow in your life, God will allow, and it will grow stronger and take root; but whatever you reject and resist through the Word of God will have no choice but to go weaker and die.* And the perfect plan of God for your life will come to pass through His Word because He is always faithful, even when we are unfaithful. Be faithful to the things of God in every way; if you love the Lord with all your being, then follow His plan and desire for your life. We cannot do it our way, no picking and choosing what we like from God's Word but totally following God's way (the only true way). We either love Him, believe in Him, do His command, or we do not. You cannot say you are a Christian but live contrary to the ways and mind of Christ and His Word. If Christ says, "Love one another." (John 13:34 NIV); He means, love one another. Allow the Holy Spirit of God to guide you into all truths, which is His Word, and let Him renew your mind to that of Christ's. We must have a renewed mind as children of God, born of the Spirit of God.

Let the Word of God be the light to your path on this dark and challenging road of life. Christ Jesus, the light of the world has come; arise and shine for the glory of the Lord is on the righteous! Let the light of God brings illumination into any darkness in your life because darkness shall never overcome the light of God. When there is light, darkness disappears; where the light of God is, no shadow of darkness will prevail. May God's light that gives life, resurrect any dead situation in your life; and may Christ shine in you and through you to others like a fragrance of sweet perfume, in His mighty name. Amen! Remember, through Christ Jesus, we now have the key to the kingdom of God, namely, the Word of Truth. The shed blood of Jesus Christ will never lose its power, and the power in the Word of God will never fail! Be steadfast in your faith because in due time, you will see the faithfulness and glory of the Lord upon your life. Do not pray about that problem anymore but pray the Word of God concerning that problem; declare the powerful Word of God in the mighty name of our Lord Jesus Christ.

THE MASTER HAS A NEED OF YOU

My entire life is a living testimony of the love, power, and faithfulness of the Lord Jesus Christ through His unchanging and powerful Word. It is an example of God's divine will and purpose for everything that He has completely and beautifully created. The Lord had a plan, a purpose, and a need for humanity even before setting out to create us. It is only by the divine plan of God, and not by my parents' desire that I am in existence, and to Him be all the glory! So, my dear friend, you were *not* born into this world by chance; you belong to the Lord Jesus and Him alone; God took His time to wonderfully and perfectly create you for a specific purpose. He made you for His pleasure and glory; it is because of His divine plan that you are here at a time like this. The Lord created you and has called you for a specific work; He has set you apart for a specific need, the very reason for which He created you in the first place. *There is a purpose and a need that only you, are assigned to fulfill in this life.* That is the reason why it may seem like you do not fit into the pattern of this world. The Lord said to young Jeremiah, "Before I formed you in the womb, I knew you, before you were born, I set you apart; I appointed you as a prophet to the nations." (Jeremiah 1:5 NIV). God has a set plan for each of us even before He forms us in the womb. The Lord's plans begin to unfold in our lives when we start to walk in His path, when we surrender to His lordship in all its entirety and live by His Word through His Spirit. Fear not, and do not be anxious about anything, but put your faith and trust in the Lord Jesus Christ and His Word. He has created us, and not we ourselves; He is our God, and we are His people created for greater task in Him and through Him. The Father is faithful to His will, through Christ Jesus our Lord.

Yes, the Lord knew you and had a plan for your life even before He formed you in your mother's womb. Just surrender your entire being—body, spirit, and soul to the Lord Jesus, and let Him have His way in you. As we stated before, my family is a typical example of God's calling and purpose. When the master has a need of you, He will set you apart from the forces of this wicked world. He will cut off all desires in you that are not of Him or pleasing in His sight, and His righteous right hand will uphold and guide you in His paths of righteousness. When you abide in the Lord Jesus, no plans of the enemy will prevail in your life because He watches over His own; He watches over those that trust in Him and in His Word. The things that tend to worry people will not bother those that are His because He gives peace to those that are in Him. When you surrender to the will of God for your life, His Holy Spirit will guide and lead you every step of the way, honoring His name in every way.

Only surrender your life totally to His lordship, so that He will fill that vacuum in your soul that nothing in this world will satisfy. That longing and hunger for the living God in your soul can only be satisfied by the Spirit of God. Allow God's will to be done in your life because many are called but few are chosen for His glory. Are you one of the few He has chosen for that specific purpose; are you one of the few He has set apart? Paul mentioned in Romans that, "For whom He foreknew, He also predestined to be conformed to the image of His Son, that He might be the firstborn among many brethren. Moreover, whom He predestined, these He also called; whom He called, these He also justified; and whom He justified, these He also glorified." (Romans 8:29 NKJV). God has entrusted to us a task that is far greater than our desires of this world, and this assignment will only succeed when we are built in Him through faith in Him. We need the Lord; people need the Lord Jesus in times like these. There is something in you that the world needs, to the glory of God the Father. God has a need for your life; creation needs that thing which the Lord has deposited in you. Stand upon the truth of Christ, and see the manifestation of the power of God displayed through His spoken Word.

IT IS GOD'S WILL THAT WE DO WELL

It is indeed the Father's will that all His children do well— spiritually as well as physically. The Father's utmost desire is that we first seek Him and His righteousness, and then everything will be added unto us (Matthew 6:33 KJV). Like any loving father would love to see his children live their lives to the full, so does our heavenly Father; it is God's desire that we live according to His will through faith in Him. God's greatest desire and reason for fearfully and perfectly creating humans is to praise Him; for us to delight in Him, and to have an everlasting relationship with Him. Whether you want to believe it or not, your life is not yours, neither is my life mine but God's; we belong to our creator, we are His, for His purpose. Christ is our all and in all, and He has promised He will never leave us nor forsake us, even when we go through our highest mountains and lowest valleys. Like the prodigal son, you may run away from God's presence, but He is your Father, and He is always there longing and waiting for your return with outstretched arms. The Father knows all your needs even before you ask Him, because He searches the heart and knows what is in your heart. He is the omniscient God who knows everything, sees all things, and to Him belongs all wisdom. Nothing is hidden from His eyes because He has complete and unlimited knowledge of all things in heaven, on earth, and under the earth.

God has perfectly created all things for His people to enjoy while we are here on earth, and that is His will and pleasure as a good Father. Look at everything around us—our planet, earth and all its fullness—the sun, the moon, the air that we breathe, the plants, the animals (great and small), the birds, the fish, and everything else that springs forth from the earth. How great and awesome is He! God knew all that we would ever need on this earth even before He made the first human; He has wonderfully and beautifully put it all in place even before forming the first Adam (man and woman). And then, God put all that He has created under our control, but we gave that authority over to the devil through the disobedience of God's command. Nevertheless, the Father's love for us did not end in the Garden of Eden; He once more clearly demonstrated His unfailing love, mercy, and grace towards us, through Christ Jesus. Christ Jesus' obedience to the will of the Father has brought us reconciliation to God. His death and resurrection has brought us peace, redemption, healing, and justification through faith in Him. We must come to the Lord in all humility and in repentance of our sinful ways. His Word tells us that, "If we confess our sins, He is faithful and just and will forgive us our sins and purify us from all unrighteousness." (1 John 1:9 NIV). My plea remains the same—if you do not know the Lord personally, ask Him now to come into your heart and let Him be the Lord of your life, and ask His Holy Spirit to take control of your life and renew your mind to that of Christ's. Trust in the Lord Jesus, trust in His name, and in His Word, because His Word is His will for your life.

Turning your back on the world and having a renewed mind through the Spirit of God, enables God's children to discern what is right and what is wrong, and to experience God's purpose for their lives. Following the plan of God for your life is what matters; nothing else in this life truly matters on the day of judgement when you stand in the presence of your creator. God is interested in your soul, that your soul prospers in His plan for your life. The Father's desire is not for any person to perish through disobedience but that we all come to His saving grace of Christ Jesus. God's plan is good, complete, flawless, and delightful and it is one that brings glory to Him. You see, my friends, God knows everything, even our deepest secrets, and He knows exactly what He will accomplish in us; He knows what we will do, and what we would not do, in any given circumstance. Thus, His plans for us will never fail when we walk in obedience to Him. God's plan and purpose for every believer is for their good, and for His glory because we are His, and He has loved us with an everlasting love. The Lord's plans are His blueprint for all humanity to follow, in order to live a godly kind of life. Our plans must be in accordance with God's plan or Word for our lives. The Bible declares that, "Many are the plans in a person's heart, but it is the LORD'S purpose that prevails." (Proverbs 19:21 NIV). And "Unless the LORD builds the house, the builders labor in vain. Unless the LORD watches over the city, the guards stand watch in vain. In vain you rise early and stay up late, toiling for food to eat—for He grants sleep to those He loves." (Psalms127:1–2 NIV). Whatever you do in this life, God must take the center stage of it, for that thing to be able to succeed; without the hand of God upon our lives and upon our daily affairs, we will not succeed to an expected end. God's will for us is always good and perfect; it is not to harm us but to give us hope, a successful life, and a future that brings glory to His name. Amen! As a good Father, it is always His desire and pleasure to give good things to His children, especially those children that love, trust, and obey Him. God's will does not fail or disappoint any one whose hope and trust are in Him. My beloved friends, endeavor to put God first in everything that you do; seek His desired plan for your life today and change your mindset as you grow and mature in the Lord.

The whole duty of every person, man, woman, or spiritual being is to reverence, worship God, and to obey His commands. All that people would ever need in this life is found in Jesus Christ; our true satisfaction comes from the Lord God, not from anything outside of the will of God. Our jobs will not satisfy us, nor any earthly accomplishments because the more we attain things, the more we want more of them; they will never fill that vacuum of satisfaction in our soul. If those things that we so desire and chase after are not of God, they will all fade away like a flower, giving us no lasting satisfaction. In fact, the Bible tells us that apart from Christ Jesus we can do nothing (John 15:5 NIV). We must earnestly seek after the knowledge of God, seek to know the Lord, and understand His fullness in everything. This will lead to the beginning of an everlasting relationship with the Father through Christ Jesus, which is God's utmost desire and will for His people. God wants our fellowship and longs for a relationship; a Father and child kind of relationship with His children through Christ.

Just imagine, if you had your children and they do not have any relationship with you whatsoever; that is never any parents' wish for their children. We must make God our number one priority in every area of our lives, in everything that we do, because His breath is in us. The importance of seeking the kingdom of God should not be taken lightly; it should always be placed at the top of every list of goals, wants, or aspirations that we could ever put together. God knows our wants are many and He has given us the key to finding everlasting satisfaction, and that is, to have a relationship with the Lord Jesus Christ and be saved. *This vicious circle of human insatiable wants will always prevail in our lives if we fail to abide by what the Word of God says.*

Our selfish ways will not lead to life eternal, most certainly not; only God's way through Christ Jesus will lead to eternal life in Him. Our ways will falsely lead us through life's challenges that appears to be holding or binding, but the result will always be disappointing, as it is not God's way or will. Our ways will not lead us to a perfect finish in life. The way of the Lord is the *only way* that we must choose and follow if we want to know and establish an everlasting relationship with the Lord and Father. There is no other way, my dear friend! You see, throughout the Bible, we have seen the importance of choosing and following the way of the Lord as exemplified by people of faith. These people of faith all realized that the only way a person ought to choose and follow, is God's way and not their own way. Christ Jesus said, "I am the way and the truth and the life. No one comes to the Father except through Me." (John 14:6 NIV). All our human knowledge will fail us; all our strength and self-reliance will take us nowhere if we fail to adhere to the way of the Lord. "For the wisdom of this world is foolishness in God's sight." As it is written: "He catches the wise in their craftiness." (1 Corinthians 3:19 NIV). Putting together all our ideologies, understanding, craftiness, and knowledge will never surmount to anything permanent outside of the will of God. We should endeavor to choose and follow the way of the Lord in everything that we pursue. The way of the Lord has been tested and tried, yet without fault; it is the only way that brings the impossible to possible through the power of His name and His spoken Word.

Let us now look at few people of God in the Bible that were diligent to the ways of God. The man Job chose and followed God's ways as stated in the Book of Job:

> But He knows the way that I take; when He has tested me, I will come forth as gold. My feet have closely followed His steps; I have kept to His way without turning aside. I have not departed from the commands of His lips; I have treasured the words of His mouth more than my daily bread. (Job 23: 10–12 NIV).

Hallelujah! May we treasure God's Word and walk in His steps and ways diligently more than anything in our lives. The psalmist, David, asked the Lord to teach him His way, saying, "Teach me Your way, LORD; lead me in a straight path because of my oppressors." (Psalms 27:11 NIV). Moses, who was called and directed by God to lead God's people out of bondage in Egypt, wrote in his second book (Exodus) saying, "If You are pleased with me, teach me Your ways so I may know You and continue to find favor with You. Remember that this nation is Your people." (Exodus 33:13 NIV). Moses realized that the only way for them to come out of bondage in Egypt, was to embark on the way of the Lord, to fervently follow God's ways set for them. *The way of the Lord is secure; the way of the Lord is perfect; the way of the Lord leads to victory because all power belongs to Him; the way of the Lord will never fail!* When you know and walk in the way of the Lord, no matter what challenges you face in this life, our faithful Lord and God will see you through them because you abide under His wings through faith in Christ Jesus. Every knee, every situation, every power, every sickness, bow at the mention of the name of Jesus Christ. Nothing is above Him or too hard for the Lord of lords and the king above all kings. David was also fully confident in choosing and following the way of the Lord. When you follow the way of the Lord, He will guide you into all truth and He will order your footsteps. Even though you may walk through the valley of the shadow of death, you shall fear no evil for the Lord will be with you; hence, the enemy will have no power over you. You shall walk and not be weary and be fruitful in all your ways in Him, because the Lord has promised He will never leave us nor forsake us. When you follow the way of the Lord, He will humble you in what is right and show you His faithfulness. The prophet Isaiah stated such:

> Although the Lord gives you the bread of adversity and the water of affliction, your teachers will be hidden no more; with your own eyes you will see them. Whether you turn to the right or to the left, your ears will hear a voice behind you, saying, "This is the way; walk in it." (Isaiah 30:20–21 NIV).

If life seems to be closing in on you, do not despair; just trust in God and follow His way, trust in His Word that will never fail. Seek answers from the Lord and not from people or things because all the wisdom and knowledge of this world are limited and foolish before God. Call on the Lord Jesus today; turn from your wicked ways and seek Him while He may be found. The Lord is waiting for you to come home, for you to turn to Him in repentance and reverence, and you shall be saved!

Friends, life is unpredictable when you are not in the Lord. We see people moving up and down and chasing after their insatiable desires. Everyone is longing for something which can never be found in any other place other than in Christ Jesus our

Lord. As we clearly mentioned, the more we achieve worldly stuff, the more we want more; we can never be satisfied without Christ Jesus, and it is only He that can satisfy the desires of our souls. When you seek God's face through the power of His Word, the revelation of His knowledge will begin to unfold in your life through the power of His Spirit in you. And with an in-depth revelation of Christ Jesus, you realize your identity, purpose, and potential in Him. With such realization, you declare the powerful Word of God in confidence whether through praise, worship, or prayer; and whatever challenge comes your way, you pray, worship, or praise your way through it because of the power in the spoken Word of God.

PRAYER

Prayer is vital as a child of God and having a consistent prayer life is part of God's will for us. As I mentioned before, we must have the eyes of faith in all areas of our lives—to believe in God and to stand on what the Word of God says concerning our lives, and that includes any situation that we may encounter. The Holy Spirit brought to remembrance the importance and power of prayer in our daily lives. In the past, God has used the prayers of ordinary people to bring about change in our world. God is looking for ordinary people like you and I, to offer prayers according to His will; prayers that will bring about effective change in the kingdom of God for His glory. God wants to use our prayers to bring down strongholds, to set the captives free, to unite the people of God, to remove the spirit of division and hate in our societies, to promote love between us, to help us stand in the day of temptation, and to help us live our daily lives. We need prayers every day of our lives, since prayer is a very powerful force that God uses for His glory. The more we devote our time to prayer, the more we mature in the Lord and become more like Him. The more we pray effectively and fervently, the more God works on our behalf and through us, with signs and wonders because there is power in the spoken Word of God!

There is power in prayer and according to the Bible, the power of prayer is simply the power of God. It is God who hears and answers prayers; we experience the power of God through prayer when we hope, believe, know, and trust that God has the power to do all things. The Father hears us when we pray persistently with thanksgiving, when we pray in faith, when we pray within the will of God (His Word) and for His glory, and when we pray from a heart that is right. The power of prayer comes from God, and when we pray, we put ourselves in contact with the almighty God who answers prayers. Our good Lord can and will answer us according to His perfect will and timing. Here are few examples of answered prayers in the Bible: Daniel was saved from the lion's den through prayer (Daniel 6:11 NKJV), Hannah was barren, and her unwavering and humble prayers caused the birth of the prophet Samuel (1 Samuel 1:20 NKJV), and Paul's prayer caused the earth to shake (Acts 16:25–26 NIV). Undoubtedly, the fervent and passionate prayers of God's righteous children can achieve much when we pray in line with God's Word, which is His will.

Praying in accordance with God's will is essentially praying in accordance with what He would want, and we can see God's revealed plan throughout the Scriptures. And if we do not know what to pray for, apostle Paul reminds us that, as God's children, we can rely on the Holy Spirit to intercede for us in accordance with God's Word; and since the Spirit of God knows the mind of God, the Spirit's prayer is always in line with the will of the Father. When we pray, we should not pray with selfish desires and wrong motives, since prayer is certainly not just about asking God for our unending needs and wants, as many may perceive prayer to be. *Prayer is having a loving dialogue with your Father in heaven; it is a relationship based on love and trust.* When we engage in prayer, we should do it in love and effectively according to the Word in order to strengthen our relationship with our Father. Let us seek to please the Lord by studying and obeying His Word, and the same God who made the sun stand still when Joshua prayed, invites us to come boldly before His throne of grace and pray with confidence and assurance in His Word (Joshua 10:12–13 NKJV). Shower your life with prayer and you will begin to experience growth in your spiritual life; and as you mature in the Lord, you begin to develop the character of Christ—love, compassion, humility, faith, self-control, and so on and so forth.

Here is an example of encouragement and prayer by the apostle Paul to the Philippians:

> I thank my God every time I remember you. In all my prayers for all of you, I always pray with joy because of your partnership in the gospel from the first day until now, being confident of this, that He who began a good work in you will carry it on to completion until the day of Christ Jesus. It is right for me to feel this way about all of you, since I have you in my heart and, whether I am in chains or defending and confirming the gospel, all of you share in God's grace with me. God can testify how I long for all of you with the affection of Christ Jesus. And this is my prayer: that your love may abound more and more in knowledge and depth of insight, so that you may be able to discern what is best and may be pure and blameless for the day of Christ, filled with the fruit of righteousness that comes through Jesus Christ—to the glory and praise of God. (Philippians 1:3–11 NIV).

If we took the time to examine this prayer in detail, we would find that Paul's focal point was his love for the Lord Jesus Christ, and to encourage the Philippians to have that same kind of love and trust for Christ. Although Paul was under house arrest (a prisoner) in Rome, yet he was full of joy and thankfulness because it was for the sake of the gospel. Paul wrote to encourage his fellow servants living in Philippi to stay strong for the sake of the gospel. Likewise, it is my sincere prayer for you to have that same kind of love and trust for the Lord Jesus Christ; and that no matter what comes your way for the sake of the gospel, through prayer and thanksgiving, you should rejoice, knowing fully well that your labor in the Lord is never in vain. Paul understood the importance of prayer and was fully aware of the power of prayer in the life of the believer. Hence, Paul's letters were rich with prayers and thanksgiving. Through prayer, and with the help of the Holy Spirit, we can be empowered to follow Christ's patterns of humility and sacrifice, and truly find joy in all circumstances. Joy in the Christian life is all about perspective. *True joy as we stated earlier is not based on circumstances but on one's relationship with God (one's right standing with the Lord). Thus, the key to lasting happiness is not found in material things of this world that fade away, but true happiness comes through a relationship with Jesus Christ.* This is the divine perspective Paul wanted to communicate to the Philippian believers and to the believers all over the world.

One way God speaks to us is through prayer. God always responds to our unselfish prayers; He moves on our behalf when we pray according to His will and for His glory. There is power in prayer and God commands us to always pray (in season and out of season), especially when we do not feel like it. The Lord calls us to boldly bring our concerns before His throne of grace, even though He knows our deepest secrets, thoughts, request, pains, joy, and triumphs; the Father still calls us to share them with Him. He longs for the communication, interaction, and love with His children. The Father wants us to call on Him in fellowship and prayer and He will answer our prayers; He also wants to share with us incredible things of His kingdom and shower us with blessings that we might otherwise have missed had we not reached out to Him through prayer. The Word tells us to, "Draw near to God, and He will draw near to you. Cleanse your hands, you sinners; and purify your hearts, your double-minded." (James 4:8 NKJV). God wants us to communicate and be close to Him always, and that can happen through prayer.

Prayer is the vehicle for daily communication with our Lord and savior Jesus Christ. Prayer is vital in the life of a believer and mentioned over 250 times in the Scriptures, as it gives us an opportunity to share all aspects of our lives with God. First, prayer gives us the chance to express our gratitude for the things God provides for us—for His faithfulness. Furthermore, prayer provides the platform for confessing our sin and asking for help in overcoming sin. Finally, prayer is an act of worship and obedience; it is a way of acknowledging who is really the *boss* of our lives. Let us endeavor to pray more than ever before, especially in times like these. *Now* is the appointed time to call on the name of the Lord Jesus Christ and be saved; *tomorrow* may be too late!

Let us look at some scriptures that will help us in our daily prayer lives: "The eyes of the LORD are on the righteous, and His ears are attentive to their cry." (Psalms 34:15 NIV). God's eyes are on those who trust in Him, on those whose hope is in His unfailing love. His ears are forever ready to listen to His children's cry because He is faithful to every promise made for those that love and trust in Him. "The name of the LORD is a strong tower; the righteous run to it and are safe." (Proverbs 18:10 NKJV). The name of Christ Jesus is *above* every other name, and at the mention of His name, every principality, power, stronghold, sickness, or any other name will surely bow because of the supernatural power in the spoken Word of the Father.

When you communicate with the Lord in prayer, trust also in Him, and rely totally on His Word. Be confident in Christ, having the understanding and belief that whatsoever He has promised He will do according to His will and purpose. In all your ways, recognize and acknowledge Christ as Lord, through your prayer, praise, thanksgiving, and worship. God is your refuge and strength; He is your shield, your light, and your salvation; and when your mind is steadfast in the Lord, you will abide in the peace of His everlasting arms. When you keep your eyes always on the Lord, and not on your circumstances or other things of this world, you will *never* be shaken or put to shame, for the Lord will sustain you. When you call on the Lord your God, He will answer you and deliver you because of His loving kindness and promises towards you. Here is our comfort from the Lord Jesus Himself saying, "Peace I leave with you; My peace I give you. I do not give to you as the world gives. Do not let your hearts be troubled and do not be afraid." (John 14:27 NIV). We have peace in Christ because of our faith in Him, so do not worry about anything but keep your eyes on Him and Him alone. Continue to walk in the way of the Lord, keep your prayer life solid and based on the Word of God.

Remember that prayer is a fundamental tool in maintaining a lasting walk and relationship with the Lord. As a child of God, you need prayer in order to survive spiritually and physically. As you dwell daily in God's presence, may you be filled with His wisdom and revelation in the knowledge of Christ Jesus. Lord, we thank you for setting us apart for Your use and glory here on earth. We fully acknowledge that You have given us this privilege not only to be set apart, but also to be Your active and joyful servants. Lord, continue to help us to fully understand the importance of being Your vessels and children, so, like apostle Paul, we would be able to say that we belong to You and have been set apart for Your glory; having the full conviction that You are the only way to peace, joy, eternal life, and enduring satisfaction. We praise you for blessing us in the heavenly realms with all spiritual blessings. Father, in the name of our Lord Jesus Christ, may you grant your people a heart flooding with your light, so that others will know and understand Your immeasurable, unlimited, and surpassing greatness of Your power, love, and hope. May your children be filled with Your presence and all Your fullness. And give us the will to claim and embrace your precious gift of abundant life in the mighty name of Jesus Christ. Amen!

THE LORD'S PRAYER

> Our Father which art in heaven, Hallowed be thy name. Thy kingdom come. Thy will be done, as in heaven, so in earth. Give us day by day our daily bread. And forgive us our sins; for we also forgive everyone that is indebted to us. And lead us not into temptation; but deliver us from evil. (Luke 11:2–4 KJV).

The Lord's prayer was taught by our Lord Jesus Christ Himself when one of His disciples asked Him to teach them how to pray. Let us reflect a little on why Christ started the prayer by referring to God as our Father; and on another occasion He also said to His disciples not to call any man on earth 'father' because we have but "One Father", who is in heaven (Matthew 23:9 NIV). God is our *only* Father who loves us with an everlasting love; Christ Jesus loves us more than we could ever imagine. He loves us with a love that is beyond human understanding, beyond every trial, temptation, and sin. The love of the Father overcomes any challenges we could ever face, but most importantly, this love gives us the boldness to come freely before His presence as His children. May you forever abide and remain in His love, and may the eyes of your understanding be enlightened to the revelation of knowing Christ. Amen!

Again, when one of His disciples asked Him to teach them how to pray, Christ Jesus started by saying "Our Father" … He had the clear vision of who God is, and He revealed to them—that the Lord God is our Father, and He is our *only Father* because He created all things, and He is above all things. Christ is above all thrones, powers, people, rulers, authority, and dominion. He is the source of all life, He has no equal, and there is none to be compared unto Him. Christ is full of mercy, grace, and loving-kindness towards us even when we do not deserve it. *God is our Father because we are from Him through His divine seed, which is His Word or Christ Jesus. When we receive God's Word of love, mercy, and salvation into our hearts, that eternal life that is in His Spirit is conceived in us, making us children of God.* When this seed of God's Word falls on good soil, on a good and upright heart that hears the Word and maintains it (keeps and acts on it), that seed produces good crop in them through their faith in the Lord and the power of the Holy Spirit. We are no longer of our human seed of fleshly birth, but of a divine and holy seed of God. And since we are not of our human seed, we are also not under any curse brought on by our human seed. We are free from any generational curse because we now belong to a divine seed of God through our faith in Christ Jesus.

> Christ redeemed us from the curse of the law by becoming a curse for us, for it is written: "Cursed is everyone who is hung on the cross or pole." He redeemed us in order that the blessings given to Abraham might come to the Gentiles through Christ Jesus, so that by faith we might receive the promise of the Spirit. (Galatians 3:13–14 NIV).

On the cross, Christ Jesus has taken upon Himself all our curses and punishment derived from our human seed of flesh.

You may ask the question; how do I know I am begotten (born) of the Father? Well, it is simple as it all starts with a choice. A free will that our loving Father has given to all humanity—a *choice to either accept Him as Lord and Father of your life or not.* Once you accept Christ as your Lord and savior, His Holy Spirit comes upon you, making you a child of God; a child born of

God Himself (born of the mind of Christ). We become children when we surrender our ways unto His ways for our lives, since we cannot say we are children of God and still hold on to the sinful desires of our flesh. Christ said to Nicodemus in the gospel of John that, "No one can see the kingdom of God unless they are born again." (John 3:3 NIV). You must be *born again*; born of water (in baptism for the forgiveness of your sins) and of the Spirit (the Spirit of God residing in you), making you a child of God. What is born of the flesh is flesh (fleshly seed and carnally minded), and what is born of the Spirit of God is Spirit (follow the things of the Spirit). When you are born of the Spirit of God, you begin to renew your mind to that of Christ's through His Word and with the help of the Holy Spirit. As you grow in the mind of Christ, you begin to develop the characteristics of Christ; to name a few: compassion, love, and humility towards others and the things of God. With Christ wholly in you, you become a slave to righteousness and no longer slave to sin.

Thank God that you have made the choice to accept our Lord Jesus as your personal savior. Again, if you have not come to this decision yet, I pray in the mighty name of Jesus Christ, that He would speak to your heart and open your spiritual eyes to His truth through the power of the Holy Spirit. May His mercy and grace be sufficient upon you when you decide to come to Him. Amen! God is our only Father who loves us regardless of our sins; His anger towards us lasts for a moment but His mercy towards us endures forever, from generation to generation. God's loving kindness is all around us because He is a good and faithful Father, who loves His children unconditionally. As our Father, He is the source of all that we would ever need, the answer to every challenge, the healer of every disease, our great judge, our provider, our comforter, our best friend, Christ is our all and in all. Let us endeavor as God's children to live a lifestyle that would reflect the image and likeness of our Father, through the power of His Word.

MEDITATE ON THE WORD OF GOD

As mentioned before, we are not here on earth by chance; we were not born by accident or because of our parent's decision. But we were fearfully and perfectly created and formed by the master creator of all things, for His glory. The Father made us to praise Him for all His acts, to worship Him out of the abundance of our love for Him. However, this God-given potential in all people can only come to fulfillment when we totally surrender to His will for our lives; when we abide in Christ Jesus and His Word abides in us. Over the years, the Lord has taught me about the importance of meditating upon His Word and feeding my spirit with the Word of the Lord. As children of God, we cannot serve the Lord without knowing who He is, what He has done, and what He is going to do through His Spirit. Knowing the Lord will lead to understanding Him and His ways, which will help us serve Him better. Contrariwise, one cannot serve God without knowing Him; thus, serving will not always lead to knowing Him. When you know and understand someone, you can relate or have a better relationship with them because you understand who they are, what they enjoy doing, what they do not like, and so on and so forth. You may ask the question, "How do I know the Lord?" We know Christ by meditating on His Word through the leadership and guidance of His Holy Spirit in us. This is indeed a choice, and we must be very intentional about it.

Meditation of the Word of God is *crucial* as children of God; feeding on the Word is the real 'Bread' or 'Food' that keeps our entire being alive and satisfied. The word 'meditate' itself comes from the Latin word "Meditari" meaning "to reflect on, to study, and to practice." Meditate in Hebrew translation gives us different words, but all have similar meaning. For example, 'Meditate' in Hebrew is "Siyach" meaning to "ponder, to converse or talk to yourself, or to utter." Regardless of the translations, we can see that meditation is a way of reflecting on the Word of God;

it is a way of thinking, muttering, studying, or declaring God's Word to oneself, in order to strengthen your spirit within. Christ Jesus mentioned that, "Man shall not live by bread alone but by every word that proceeds from the mouth of God." (Matthew 4:4 NKJV). We need the Word of God on our lips, in our spirit, and in our soul in order to live the life that God has intended us to live in Christ. We need the Word of God to take root in us and eventually bear fruits that will last as the evidence of His Spirit in us: love, joy, peace, forbearance, kindness, goodness, faithfulness, gentleness, and self-control (Galatians 5:22-23 NIV). These qualities of the Father will be evidenced in us when we are truly born of the Spirit of God. The Lord God, in Joshua 1:8, commanded young Joshua to meditate upon His Word day and night, and to observe to do all that is written in it, in order to have a good success and be prosperous. The reason being that the Word of God is the key to the knowledge of God; it is the blueprint, power, and weapon for the believer in Christ Jesus. God's Word is eternal, trustworthy, and stands forever; the Word restores and revives the soul, body, and spirit. God's Word gives joy to the heart and light to the eyes; it is life itself, and full of creative power; *the Word is Christ Jesus Himself.* With the Word, we praise the name of the Lord God in worship and adoration, and we also overcome the works of the devil. King David mentioned, "I have hidden your Word in my heart that I might not sin against you." (Psalm 119:11 NIV). When you store up God's Word in your heart and spirit, you will be able to withstand every temptation from the devil using that Word of God. It is only through the Word of God that you can overcome the devil's schemes. As Christ overcame the devil with the Word saying, "It is written..." (Matthew 4:1–11 NIV); so, shall we also. We need to have the revelation of the power in the Word of God and stand firm on it, believing what God has said in its entirety; and we must comprehend the weight of God's majesty, love, and authority in His Word as children of God.

Meditate upon the Word of God so that you can grow spiritually and be strong on the inside, strong in your relationship with the Lord Jesus; and your way will be made prosperous. As you become acquainted with the Word of God, begin to declare it into your real life's situations because there is life changing power in the spoken Word of God. "The entrance of Your words gives light; it gives understanding to the simple." (Psalm 119:130 NKJV). When the Word of God enters a good heart that accepts it, it brings forth light, which unfolds the knowledge and understanding of God in them. The Word of God is the light in this dark world and in your life; it drives away darkness because the light will always overcome darkness. The Word is a guide to your path in life; it will guide you into all truth. Strive to meditate upon God's Word and remember that everything was created through the spoken Word of God. Therefore, in the same way, the Word of God that you speak has life and power to create wonders and change lives. This empowerment can only be manifested through meditation and being obedient to God's Word. God will never deny Himself—He is His Word; so, feed on it.

PUT ON THE FULL ARMOR OF GOD

Meditating on God's Word will enable us to withstand attacks from the evil one. It is in the Word that lies the source of long life, good success, prosperity, hope, and eternity. The Word of God is our weapon against the evil forces of this dark world. Even though we understand that Christ has delivered us from the power of darkness through His obedience on the cross, we still need to walk in that truth by taking a stand in the Word and in the authority given to us over the power of darkness. Salvation does not mean automatic freedom; salvation gives us power over the darkness, bringing glory to God in it and through it. As we go through our daily lives, we must always be mindful about the schemes of the devil and remember that the devil's main purpose is to kill, steal, and destroy God's children in every way possible. We understand by now that from the beginning, the devil has always desired worship and he will do anything and everything to get worship instead of God, who is worthy of all praise, worship, and adoration. The devil will even try to take away our freedom to worship God by constantly looking for whom he may overcome and destroy. We are constantly faced with the devil's schemes and devices but thank God for the Word of God; thank God for His living Word with which we can overcome the evil one. There is victory in the Word of God!

There is power in the Word of God and therefore we as believers must not only meditate on it, but also put on the whole armor of God as our constant spiritual clothing. The apostle Paul explains this process of preparation, which is vital for our existence in Ephesians 6:

> Finally, be strong in the Lord and in His mighty power. Put on the full armor of God, so that you can take your stand against the devil's schemes. For our struggle is not against flesh and blood, but against the rulers, against the authorities, against the powers of this dark world and against the spiritual forces of evil in the heavenly realms. (Ephesians 6:10–12 NIV).

In verse 12, we are told that our battle is against spiritual forces and so we must equip ourselves with the spiritual armor of God. Unfortunately, the despairing situation of unbelievers is that they have no spiritual intelligence, and cannot in any way even be aware of the spiritual forces of darkness that entangle them in a stronghold. But as children of God, we are spiritually alive and able to discern the power of the spiritual realm that is coming against us. Moreover, we have the power to nullify these forces in the mighty name of Jesus Christ our Lord through the power of the Holy Spirit. Hence, we must be fully clothed in God's armor.

We must clothe ourselves with the person of truth as much as with the Word of truth (Christ Jesus). The genuineness of God's Word is the reality of Christ Jesus in the flesh. In other words, *if we believe Christ Jesus was here on earth as God in the flesh, as the Son of God, then we are compelled to believe no less in God's Word that we now read as Scriptures.* When we are not covered with God's Word, we are obviously susceptible to attacks. Christ Jesus is God's living Word; it is His life working through us, which is His Word. We must endeavor to clothe ourselves with the *person of truth*, and when we are clothed with the *truth*, Christ Jesus is seen through our actions, and the Word working in us reminds the devil that Christ Jesus' victory still holds now and forever. Our source of strength is God's Word against which the devil has no victory. When we stand against the enemy with God's Word, it is like the manifested appearance of Christ Jesus, for we can *never separate Christ and His Word.* God's Word working in us is the certainty to the devil that Jesus' victory over the world and over him is forever more. When we clothe our lives with God's Word, our weaknesses become God's strength and our eternal victor is manifested and glorified amongst us.

GREATEST SUCCESS

Earthly success in this life is something that many people try to achieve during their lifetime, falsely hoping that it will bring them happiness. But earthly goals (money, fame, power, accomplishment, human wisdom, and so on and so forth) will not by any means bring happiness. *True success is not the obtaining of material things of this world; it is not about things of the flesh, but true success is you being able to understand and do what God has created you to do, for His glory.* You may then ask, "What do I have to do to discover what I was created to do?" The Word of God tells us that

God has given us everything pertaining to life and godliness in His Word (2 Peter 1:3 NKJV). The Word as I mentioned earlier is the plan of how the creator God intended you and I to live here on earth. The Word tells us to seek first the kingdom of God and His righteousness, and all other things shall be added (Matthew 6:33 NKJV). We must seek God and His righteousness by having the mind of Christ Jesus; the whole character of Christ in us that seeks after knowing and pleasing God. In the kingdom of God, success is not measured by the things of this world, but by a person's relationship with God, who they are in Him and their willingness to do the will of God for His glory. *A life that is totally submissive and devoted to God will bring true joy. Obedience to the will of God is the greatest success in this world.* So, *do not store up for yourselves treasures on this fleeting earth, but store up for yourselves treasures in heaven through faith in Christ Jesus and His Word.* And try also not to follow the ways and patterns of this world but grow in the mind of Christ Jesus through His Word and Holy Spirit. Your daily work with the Lord will increase your faith and trust in Him, but disobedience will lead to unhappiness and an unfulfilled life. A life that seeks the Lord Jesus is a life destined for glory. *Disobedience to the things of God will lead to destruction; and God will sometimes cause things to happen as a way of humbling His children—until we become obedient to His will for our lives.* God demonstrated His humbling with the Israelites in the wilderness on their way to the Promised Land, "He humbled you, causing you to hungry and then feeding you with manna, which neither you nor your ancestors had known, to teach you that man does not live on bread alone but on every Word that comes from the Mouth of God." (Deuteronomy 8:3 NIV). The Father has a way of humbling His children who detour off His track, in order to get their full attention once more. God's Word is the *true bread* of life and His Spirit the *true living water*; without such, we will surely die—spiritually and then physically.

Jonah wanted to go his own way instead of listening to God's instructions; God caused a big fish to swallow him, which made him to finally surrender (Jonah 1:17 NIV). Why do people have to wait until something bad happens before surrendering to God? Put your trust in the Lord, in His name, and in His Word; your trust should not be in your possessions, in temporary things of this world, but your trust must be in the Lord your God and Him alone. For whatever the Lord does, or has done, lasts forever—His ways, His Word, His favor, His blessings, and His love are eternal. Your greatest success is in the Lord Jesus Christ; you, being that man or woman for which you were created to be. Let your mind be that of Christ Jesus and your words in accordance with God's *never changing* Word. Abide in the Lord, in His Word, and let His Holy Spirit abide in you and through you.

We praise You O Lord God almighty, among the nations; we sing of Your power, mercy, grace, loving-kindness, and faithfulness among Your people. For mighty are the works of Your hands both great and small. Who is like You, O Lord or who is Your equal? Who can be compared or likened unto You O most high? You are greatly to be feared and reverenced in the assembly of the saints. Your love reaches to the heavens; it is deeper than the seas, it flows to the lowest valleys and to the highest mountains of our lives. You have established Your faithfulness in the heavens; it also surrounds You and reaches to the skies from generation to generation. The heavens and earth are all Yours, the world and all its fullness. Righteousness and justice are the foundation of Your throne; mercy and truth go before Your face. You are worthy of our praise O Lord God for all your acts, and we worship and adore You out of the abundance of our love for You. Day after day, we will exalt Your holy name that is above every other name, and may Your glory O Lord be magnified in all the earth, even as you bless the works of our hands. In your mighty name Lord Jesus. Amen!

We must worship God because *it is our duty.* God created us in His image and likeness to worship Him and declare His praise; the Father created us (both male and female) out of the abundance of His love, for His pleasure and glory. We belong to Him and Him alone; all people belong to God—to serve Him in the beauty of His holiness. As a result, God has created and given us everything we would ever need here on earth. From the moment we are born to the day we leave this earth in death, everything physically and spiritually that we would ever need and want is found on this planet earth. The Father deserves our praise for all that He has done, and our worship for the love that we have for Him. We worship Him not because of material gain or for His blessings that He bestows upon us, but because of who He is. Have a relationship with God for such is His desire; He longs for your *heart,* for your *fellowship.* The Lord is not interested in your services or your offerings because the whole earth and everything in it belong to Him; rather He is most interested in your spiritual growth and a relationship with Him that leads to eternal life in Him. What God desires is your whole heart, your soul, and your mind; one that seeks after Him in a true relationship. *All people are responsible and accountable to God concerning their lives; there is a day when we will all stand before the Father and give an account of our lives.* King Solomon received the revelation saying, "Now all has been heard; here is the conclusion of the matter: Fear God and keep His commandments, for this is the duty of all mankind. For God will judge every deed, including hidden things, whether good or bad." (Ecclesiastes 12:13 NIV). The *only* duty of all humans, the only reason for which we were created, is to worship and praise the Lord God.

People were created by God and for God; to worship and give Him all the glory, *period!* Let us go back to the very beginning in the Garden of Eden, where it all started. The Word of God tells us that God completed His creation of the heavens and the earth in all their vast array. He also created the first humans (male and female) to take care of everything He had wonderfully created. And in the cool of the day, God would walk in the garden to fellowship with them (Genesis 1, 2 and 3 NIV). The Father created us to rule over and take care of all that the He had created—the fish in the sea, the birds in the sky, all the livestock, all the wild animals, and all the creatures that move upon the face of the earth. God blessed the people and commanded them to be fruitful and increase in number; to fill the earth and subdue it, and to rule over all the creatures that He had created. God also commanded the man and woman to freely eat from any tree in the garden, but not to partake from the tree of the knowledge of good and evil, for if they ever did, they would certainly die (Genesis 2:16–17 NIV). Did they obey God's command? No, and thus, their disobedience to God's command from the beginning brought about the fall of all humanity (sin). The cunning devise of the devil, led to the loss of the authority given to humans by God, which is to rule and reign. Nevertheless, we thank God that through the death and resurrection of our Lord Jesus Christ, that authority and sin has been atoned for in full on the cross.

Our obligation now is to commit our ways unto the Lord, and trust in Him, and He shall bring our desires to pass, desires that bring glory to Him. When we talk about "Commit," we do not merely mean being involved, but 'totally giving our all' (total surrender) to the Lord Jesus Christ over our lives; *being dead to ourselves*—no more about us but all about the Lord Jesus and His ways in us (we are out of the equation). Let us give a simple analogy using an everyday activity of an egg and a piece of bacon on a breakfast plate. The chicken was involved by producing her egg, but the pig was fully committed by giving its all (its life); in other words, the pig had to die for us to enjoy the bacon. This is what it takes to be committed; we must give up our ways, our lives, in order to gain life (the life of Christ) more abundantly in Him. We must first, have the revelation of His knowledge and then delight in the Lord, in order to commit unto Him; this leads to true worship. *Knowledge leads to understanding, and understanding yields delight and worship.* We quite understand that when a person delights in something or someone, they certainly want to be always with that thing or person. When you delight, you want to please greatly; you have great pleasure or even find happiness with that thing or someone. Thus, it is, and even more so with the Lord; when you have the true knowledge, high gratification, and love for your creator and savior, you are always eager and longing for that moment with Him in worship and fellowship. You become drawn unto the Lord as you begin to fall in love with Him leading to true worship, and an eternal love relationship through the power of His Holy Spirit. As a result, you commit your life unto the Lord, and you trust in Him; knowing fully well with all confidence that He is faithful to every promise He has made concerning you in His Word.

Obedience to the Word of God and to His Holy Spirit is true success, and an open door to God's promises. "If you are willing and obedient, you shall eat the good of the land; but if you refuse and rebel, you shall be devoured by the sword; for the mouth of the LORD has spoken." (Isaiah 1:19 NKJV). If we are willing to seek the Lord Jesus with all our hearts, we will find Him. *Do not follow an organization, a church, an ideology, a religion, a pastor, or religious leader, but seek to follow the Lord God almighty; have a relationship with the Lord Jesus, abide in His Word, and live according to the leadership of His Holy Spirit.* Follow the Lord Jesus Christ and you will live more abundantly in the Lord; anything apart from the Lord Jesus Christ and His Holy Spirit is *temporal* and *dead*. Outside of the true Word of God, the name of Jesus Christ, and His Holy Spirit is just a '*dead worship with no power.*' Hence in these 'dead' gatherings (in the name of God but far from His truth and Spirit of God), there is no manifestation of the presence and power of God; no miracles in such a mist because miracles from the Lord follow His spoken Word. When the spoken Word of God comes forth (Thus says the Lord), it is followed by signs and wonders; the Word and the Spirit are one, they go together in the mighty name of Jesus Christ our Lord. Keep God's Word in your mouth, meditate on it day and night; and feed on it in every situation. Just as Joshua advised the Israelites, "Keep this Book of the Law always on your lips; meditate on it day and night, so that you may be careful to do everything written in it. Then you will be prosperous and successful." (Joshua 1:8 NIV). So, speak the Word out in faith to the glory and pleasure of the Father. Praise and worship the Lord in obedience because it is our duty; it is the reason for which we were created.

WHAT IS WORSHIP?

Worship is a concept that is talked about all the time in the body of Christ and even in our secular world. But the worship we want to discover is that of the creator God, who made all things for His glory and pleasure. Worship is the extreme expression of our love for God, as we reverence, surrender, and enthrone the Lord. Unlike praise, which we do unto the Lord for all His wonderful works; we worship out of the abundance of our love for the Lord God. Worship is an extreme form of love expressed in different ways; worship is love beyond measure, crazy kind of love for the Lord God, it is the love of Christ in our hearts that compels worship. Therefore, true worship is Christ in you manifested in every area of your life; it is doing the right thing when you do not feel like it, when all is against you, but you still worship anyway—*worship is a duty.* When you truly find Christ Jesus, worship becomes the lifestyle of love because worship is what defines and humbles the believer to the presence of God. As we continuously worship God, He also draws closer to us and does what only He can do in us and through us. This love of God in the believer is displayed in every area of their lives; it is this worship in you that will cause you to love your neighbor and treat others with love and respect. God is a God of worship because God is love and worship is love; and the Father desires our worship as He dwells in the praises of His people. The Word of God tells us that the hosts of heaven never stop worshipping God:

> Each of the four living creatures had six wings and was covered with eyes all around, even under its wings. Day and night they never stop saying: "HOLY, HOLY, HOLY IS THE LORD GOD ALMIGHTY, WHO WAS, AND IS, AND IS TO COME." Whenever the living creatures give glory, honor, and thanks to Him who sits on the throne and who lives forever and ever, the twenty-four elders fall down before Him who sits on the throne and worship Him who lives forever and ever. They lay their crowns before the throne and say: "You are worthy, our Lord and God, to receive glory and honor and power, for you created all things, and by your will they

were created and have their being." (Revelation 4:8–11 NIV).

Worship is part of the fiber of our being as humans because we were created in the image of God, who is Himself worship and dwells in it. We were created to give God all the glory, honor, and thanks due to His name. *God is only interested in our praise, in our worship, in our fellowship, in our heart, and in our total surrender to Him. The Lord God is not interested in buildings, nor our money, or our services or effort, but He is after our heart of worship and adoration towards Him.* God wants to move in your life and show you great and mighty things that you know not of. He wants to change everything in you and around you, but this can only happen through worship— through a heart of love, gratitude, and humility. Let every aspect of your life be of worship to the Lord God almighty.

HOW DO WE WORSHIP?

How we worship God is a very important and crucial topic in the body of Christ, and it is a message that needs our full attention and understanding. Many Christians in our generation believe that they can worship God in any way—*their own way.* When a person is truly in Christ and filled with the Spirit of God, they are dead to themselves; it is no more their old ways but Christ fully living in them—the ways of Christ. Let us go back to our manual, which is the Word of God. Why did Christ Jesus make this statement saying, "Yet a time is coming and has now come when the true worshipers will worship the Father in the Spirit and in truth, for they are the kind of worshipers the Father seeks." (John 4:23 NIV). So, if there is a *'true way to worship,'* then all other ways must be *wrong* (not of God), and the worshipers are also false in their own ways. Worship in spirit and in truth goes much deeper; it does not mean just going to church once or twice a week, singing some songs, and saying a few prayers.

True worshipers must worship the Father in His Spirit and in His truth (Christ is the truth), because God is a Spirit and seeks such worship. Worship in spirit simply means worshipping as led by the Spirit of God in you, giving God all your love, all your being in worship—with all your heart, spirit, mind, strength, and soul because of the love that you have for Him. This is only done when your spirit and soul are renewed by the Holy Spirit of God, when your spirit is obedient, and in line with the desires of the Spirit of God. Since worship is an extreme expression of love, the love of Christ in a believer, it must also be manifested in every area of our lives and in different forms. Worship in truth is worshipping God according to His Word (The Bible), in totality, because the Word is truth and believers must live in accordance with the Word of God (John 17:17 NIV). A true worshipper is true to Christ Jesus and His Word in every way, and does not fake any area of his/her life to please people or religious standards. God is not looking for our perfection because He perfects us, but He wants to see the genuineness of our hearts towards Him, which is true worship according to His Word. As God is His word—true in all His ways, so must His worshippers be. How we worship God always starts with faith in Him; then our worship becomes the action of our faith (our love for Him). The Word of God tells us that, "And without faith it is impossible to please God, because anyone who comes to Him must believe that He exists and that He rewards those who earnestly seek Him." (Hebrews 11:6 NIV). You must first, believe that there is a God in heaven who created *all* things (both visible and invisible) for His praise, glory, and worship, and that He also created people for His pleasure and praise. We are all His people, whether you want to believe it or not; we came from glory and unto glory we shall return.

The way we present our bodies when we come before the presence of God is another form of worship. Apostle Paul encourages us saying: "Therefore, I urge you, brothers and sisters, in view of God's mercy, to offer your bodies as a living sacrifice, holy and pleasing to God—this is our true and proper worship." (Romans 12:1 NIV). Present yourself in an appropriate manner that is worthy of the gospel when you come before your creator; whatever you do, let it be pleasing in the sight of the Lord. When you are born of the Spirit of God, you do mind the things of the Spirit such as self-control. We represent the Lord Jesus in whatever we say or do, since our actions reflect our faith and reverence of the Lord.

Another form of worship is exaltation, praise, and thanksgiving to God for all that He has done and continues to do, as the Holy Spirit gives you utterance according to His Word. Psalms 100 tells us to, "Enter His gates with thanksgiving and His courts with praise; give thanks to Him and praise His name." (Psalms 100:4 NIV). You could start worshipping like this: *Father, I worship and exalt You; I praise Your holy name because You are great, and greatly to be praised! There is none like You, and Your ways no one can fathom. You are the alpha and the omega, the beginning and the end of everything, and so on and so forth as the Holy Spirit gives you the utterance.* Tell God who He is, proclaim His attributes, His loving-kindness, and mercy according to His Word.

Worship the Lord with shouts of joy and singing, and with instruments. The psalmist tells us to, "Shout for joy to the LORD, all the earth. Worship the LORD with gladness; come before Him with joyful songs." (Psalm 100:1–2 NIV). Worship with gladness and gratitude to God for His goodness and faithfulness towards you, for the free and vital things in life that we all take for granted, and yet He remains faithful to His Word and to all His creation. The Lord longs for your voice of singing and praise unto Him; do not say I cannot sing because that would not be true. Every person created in the image and likeness of the Father could sing because our maker, who is God, *sings!* So, yes, you can sing, my dear friends, because you are wonderfully and perfectly made for His glory.

As we are led by the Spirit of God, we worship with hands lifted, knees bowed down, or even prostration before the throne of God. These actions all symbolize our love, total humility, surrender, powerlessness, awe, and reverence to God's surpassing greatness, power, and majesty. Our entire body is for the Father's worship and praise; wonderfully and perfectly made for His pleasure. Worship the Lord with every fiber of your being because He deserves your every praise; for great is the Lord and worthy of praise! He is the God, who holds your life in His hand, who knows your tomorrow, who knows every thought of your mind, and knows what goes on in your heart. He holds all things together by His mighty working power. How great Thou art, O Lord!

We also worship God through our words and thoughts. Our everyday words and thoughts should be edifying in every way, full of truth, encouragement, faith, hope, and love of the Lord Jesus Christ. What you say affects you and others around you; the right word can be life changing to someone. "Finally, brothers and sisters, whatever is true, whatever is noble, whatever is right, whatever is pure, whatever is lovely, whatever is admirable—if anything is excellent or praiseworthy—think about such things." (Philippians 4:8 NIV). When your thoughts are in line with the Word of God, only enriching and praiseworthy words will proceed out of you. Hence, your worship will lead to life changing experiences in all areas of your life, and you will begin to live a lifestyle of worship. Let our faith in Christ Jesus be manifested in our worship to Him, with all that we are (body, spirit, and soul).

WHY DO WE WORSHIP?

Love is what compels us to worship God; because of the love that we have for Him, which comes through salvation (faith in Christ Jesus), is one of the main reasons why we worship our Lord God almighty. But we must never forget the fact that, it is our duty to worship God since He created us to worship Him.

Every year in the United States we celebrate July 4th, which is our nation's Independence Day, and we rejoice as a nation under God for our freedom. This is all good but the greatest freedom, my dear friends, is that of the freedom of our spirit and soul from eternal damnation through the sacrifice of Jesus Christ our Lord. *Salvation is our greatest freedom, and it must be appreciated and valued more than anything because we have been bought with a high price, which is the precious blood and life of Christ Jesus.* And worship is part of our blueprint because God Himself is worship (love) and resides in the praises of His people. When we are filled with the love, fullness, and revelation of the knowledge of God, we would have no option but to worship Him in love, reverence, and awe. We were created to worship our creator, and our worship of God is our response to His love because He first loved us, even before He laid the foundations of the earth. The Lord has loved us with an eternal love through Christ Jesus our Lord; He had a plan for His people even before He created us or formed us in the womb. The Lord is the great king of all the universe, all-powerful, sovereign, most holy, and just God, who reached out to us in love through His Son to restore us back to Himself. Christ has paid in full our debt, He has served completely the sentence that we deserved for sin, and He has won the battle over sin, the devil, and every enemy of our lives. Now let us walk in confidence of Christ's victory even through our worship.

Worship is the expression of our faith and relationship with God. The Bible tells us that, "As the body without the spirit is dead, so faith without deeds is dead." (James 2:26 NIV). Worship is a way of showing forth our love, faith, and fellowship towards the master of our being, the one who sustains all things, the one who holds our lives in His hand, and who wakes us up right on time each morning. The Lord is worthy of your worship and praise for all that He is and all that He has done! Therefore, worship is our duty and the right thing to do because God's breath is in us. Worship pleases God, and not our sacrifices or offerings but our broken spirits and repentant hearts of love before the Lord. We must worship with all our being (spirit, soul, and body), worship as led by the Holy Spirit of God, and according to His Word (the truth). *When we worship God, He moves on our behalf over the enemy; He keeps us under the protection of His mighty hands.* When we worship the Lord, we thwart Satan's plan against us and dethroned his kingdom. Remember, Satan's goal is to keep us from worshiping the Lord, and to draw our focus and attention away from God. Our worship is the weapon that breaks every chain and bondage in our lives. That is why worship is not a religious ceremony on a Sunday morning or Wednesday evening; worship is a lifestyle of love in the believer, an expression of an eternal love relationship between two lovers—God and you. We show forth love (worship) in every area of our lives and in different expressions as led by the Holy Spirit, and according to the Word of God. Worship is love and God is love!

WHERE DO WE WORSHIP?

As I was reflecting on this concept of where to worship God, the Holy Spirit led me straight to the longest conversation Christ Jesus ever had. His conversation with the Samaritan woman in the gospel of John, Chapter 4, which led to the woman's salvation and the truth about the right place of worship. According to this passage, the Samaritan woman was certainly worried about her salvation and the right place of worship. Her ancestors worshiped on the mountain, but the Jews maintained that the place of worship must be in Jerusalem. But Christ made it clear to her that the place of worship is neither on the mountain nor in Jerusalem, but in her. In other words, the place of worship is no longer as important as it was in Old Testament times because, as children of God, we are now the temple of God, and the Spirit of God lives in us (1 Corinthians 3:16 NKJV). Worshiping of God is now a continuous lifestyle or journey that goes beyond set days and times; worship is now practiced anywhere, at any time, and in different forms. This, however, does not exclude going to church for worship and fellowship, but it simply means that we have no restriction of place to worship God. We can now worship God anywhere because we know Him as Father through our adoption as children of God, children born of the Spirit of God through our faith in Christ Jesus. Worship is a deeper expression of our appreciation and love that we have for the Lord Jesus, for *all* that He is, *all* that He has done, and continues to do for us. It is our continuous song and melody for the lover of our soul and the reason of our existence, conveyed in all areas of our lives.

Again, worship is not 20 minutes singing of songs and then we expect the presence of God to move in our midst; it is not about musicians, but it is all about true worshipers that will worship the Father in all sincerity, with all their being, as led by the Holy Spirit, and according to His Word. Our worship is a demonstration of our relationship with the Lord Jesus; it is not about following a church group, an organization or a religious person. Worship is about adhering to the true Word of God, which brings forth true worship. *True worshippers embrace or live by the Word and the Spirit of God. If anyone turns from the Word of God and His Spirit by following a church or an organization, that man or woman dies spiritually (separation from God).* Do not allow anything or anyone to replace the Word of God and the Spirit of the Father in you. A heart full of worship is better to lead worship than the most sophisticated orchestra. God is not impressed with numbers, buildings, or services, but He is impressed with a sincere heart and a penitent spirit longing for His intimacy and love. The Lord is after your heart, and a personal relationship with you.

Worship comes from within; it is a deep reaction to God's action of His love for us through Christ Jesus. This response of our love in return is expressed in our endless actions of worship in all areas of our lives, and this is certainly not limited to any place or building. Our whole being is a living sacrifice of worship (of love) because in Christ we live and move and have our entire existence. Wherever you are and in whatever you do, know that God's Spirit is in you (child of God) because you are His temple, and He does not reside in buildings but in hearts of ordinary people like us, who believe and trust in Him. As a loving Father, He longs for our fellowship, our adoration, our praise, our appreciation, and our love. Just call on the Lord Jesus today with all your heart in worship and He will answer you; His eyes are always on the righteous, and His ears are attentive to their cry (Psalms 34:15 NIV).

THE BENEFITS OF WORSHIP

As we grow and mature in the Lord, we come to realize that worship is vital in the life of a believer in Christ Jesus; it is the foundation upon which we build a lifelong journey of relationship with God our Father. As we have learned, worship is our response (of love) to God's everlasting love towards us. As we mentioned, our worship to God is the demonstration of our love, faith, and appreciation of Him. The Father seeks our worship not for His advantage or profit but for our benefit in every area of our lives. *God does not need us, but He wants us through our worship and relationship with Him. On the other hand, we need God more than the air we breathe or our next heartbeat; we need Him for our entire existence (in every step along the way).*

First, we need to clarify the fact that our worship of God does not change who God is, but it changes everything about us. God is omnipresent, omnipotent, and omniscient; He is the almighty, all sufficient, and supreme, who owns and rules all of creation, and *needs nothing.* When our worship comes before the Lord and He inhabits our praise and worship, life changing experience is bound to happen. It is through worship that everything flows— healing, restoration, comfort, renewing of the mind, salvation, forgiveness, and deliverance. Whatever need you may have my dear friends, just begin to worship the Father through His Word, and see those shackles drop off and disappear in the mighty name of Jesus.

Worship brings us intimately closer to the presence of God and as we draw closer to Him, as His Holy Spirit begins to unravel deeper things to us about the kingdom of God. Then we begin to realize the reality, greatness, and love of God through His Son towards us. King David understood this revelation about the power of worship, and as a result, he worshipped God in every circumstance. During his battles, in personal sin, when in distress and apprehension, in sickness, or in pain; David faithfully worshipped God in them and through them all; he had a sincere heart and love for the Lord. Begin to declare the life changing Word of God in worship and see the power of the living Word change you from the inside out.

Worship is the key that releases God's blessings upon His children. Again, our worship is an act of obedience to the voice of God through His Holy Spirit at work in us. Our obedience to the Lord and His Word is better than any amount of sacrifice, and it brings forth God's hand of protection and provision. That is why the Word of God tells us that, "Blessed is the nation whose God is the LORD, the people He chose for His inheritance." (Psalms 33:12 NIV). When a nation's eyes are poised on the living God, His Word, and His Spirit, that nation prospers in every way (both spiritually and physically). These blessings from the Lord will lead to testimonies and boasting about the Lord our God for all that He has done. Worship empowers the believer to realize their authority in the Lord over the kingdom of darkness that tends to stand in the way of God's children. Principalities, spiritual wickedness, and chains in your life are broken in the mighty name of Jesus when you come before God's presence in worship. Worship is a must, just like you must be born again in order to enter the kingdom of God. When we accept the fact that worship is a 'must', that it is a command, and a privilege, we will begin to experience the glory and outpouring of God's presence in our midst. As we worship, supernatural changes and blessings will take place in all areas of our lives, to the glory and praise of God. As God is His Word (true in all aspect), so must His worshippers be (in sincerity of heart and spirit). When we are filled with God's Word, it is demonstrated by the outburst of His worship in us.

Worship is a lifestyle of continuous love and adoration of the God we know as Lord of all. *When you worship in ignorance, it becomes religion but when you worship in love and with the knowledge of Christ Jesus, it becomes true worship.* God longs for your continuous fellowship, so your worship is no longer defined as an act but a lifestyle of gratitude, love, adoration, reverence, and faith. We are indeed privileged to have such an intimate relationship with the eternal king of all kings, the immortal, and the invisible God. Let us allow our entire being to worship the giver and sustainer of every breath. Have a lifestyle of worship and reverence towards God because He cares for you. Know that God's Word is His divine will and blueprint for your life, and that, there is power in the spoken Word of God, in the mighty name of Jesus Christ our Lord!

May the joy of the Lord be your strength as you live a life worthy of the gospel, seeking His face, and walking in His glorious light which He has graciously bestowed upon you through faith in Him. May your life be pleasing in His sight, bearing fruit in every good work, growing in the knowledge of God, being strengthened with all power according to His glorious might, and giving joyful thanks to the Father. May the Holy Spirit be your guide, teacher, and helper in this eternal journey in the mighty name of our Lord Jesus. Father, in the name of our Lord Jesus Christ, give Your people, O Lord, the peace that surpasses all knowledge and understanding for Your mighty name's sake and for Your glory. That we may walk and believe in Your Word and be moved by the power of Your Holy Spirit. We come against every sickness, every challenge, every pain, and every situation that tends to raise itself against God's children, to flee right now in Jesus' mighty name. We declare the peace of God in homes, hearts, and minds of your children in Your name, Lord Jesus, and may every Word of God declared come alive in us and through us, to the glory of God the Father, now and forever more. In Your mighty name Lord Jesus, we pray. Amen!

IF YOU CAN BELIEVE IT, YOU CAN HAVE IT

Understanding this revelation of *'Believing in God'*, will change your life forever for the master's glory. Believing in God is a concept that is mostly confused with having faith in God. Even though both words are very much linked or interrelated, they are somehow different. Since we have talked on faith, we will not focus more on it but rather go onto what 'Believing in God' is all about. We know that faith is the confidence we have in who God is, what He has done, what He is going to do, His power, love, grace, and mercy. This assurance in God comes through hearing of the Word or the good news of salvation of Christ Jesus our Lord. Faith brings forth our assurance in God, which sometimes comes through our personal experiences with Him. God then becomes that *element or ingredient (substance)* of all that we will ever hope for, who is the evidence of the unseen—including our desires. We develop a deeper understanding and knowledge of who God is by spending time with Him—through reading of His Word, prayer, testifying of His goodness and faithfulness, and through His entire creation. We know that prophets of old believed God, they lived by faith, and died in faith; they had total confidence in every spoken Word of God. As a result, the Lord God worked with them in great display of miraculous wonders; God honored their faith in Him through miracles that accompanied them in words and in deeds.

The first step in having an everlasting relationship with God is believing in Him—believing in what He has said in His Word, and in what He has done on the cross. You must believe that God is a Spirit and that He exists in everything He has created— visible, invisible, great, and small. God's divine attributes are in everything He has perfectly created; and so, people have no excuse for not worship or doubt of His existence. You must also believe with every fiber of your being that; God is a rewarder of those that wholeheartedly seek Him. He is a good Father and takes pleasure in doing good to His beloved children, those that earnestly love, trust, and seek to please Him.

Believing in God is the action or choice you make when you have total confidence in God and His Word. *If you can believe it, you can have it!* When you believe in God, your faith will be transformed into actions. You can say that you have faith in God and His Word but if you do not totally believe in God with all might, body, soul, and spirit to the point that ultimately compels and puts your faith into action, then you do not truly believe in Him. Believe yields forth *action*; we love because He is love and He has first loved us. *We live according to Christ's example.* The Bible tells us that, "Abraham believed God, and it was credited to him as righteousness." (Romans 4:3, NIV). Abraham developed a holy fear of God through his belief in God; He understood that all things were possible with God and that God is faithful to His Word. Abraham did not consider his condition, he did not take into consideration his age, or time. He heard the voice of God, believed in who God is, what God has done, and what the sovereign one can do. His eyes were on the supernatural greatness and power of the living God. And, as a result, Abraham was able to walk with God in obedience without wavering in his faith. *Believing is the choice one makes*; the choice to either love God and adhere to His commands or not. It is a choice that one must make; your parents or family cannot make it for you but you; they can show you or usher you into the truth, but you *must partake by yourself;* it is an act of obedience and faith that you must make. You cannot say you have faith in God but do not believe, respond, or act upon His Word. Your ways, lifestyle, and obedience declare your love and faith. Faith and belief go together; you move as the Spirit of God leads you. You must live in obedience to God's Word as a child of God. *Do not try to figure out God because you can never fathom His ways; just move (believe) in the power of His might according to His Word and Spirit.*

Sometimes moving in the power of God can be daunting or can seem foolish to them that are perishing, but we know that the gospel of Christ Jesus is the power of God unto salvation for *everyone* who believes (Romans 1:16 NIV). So, set your eyes on the keeper of your soul, the one who holds your life in the palm of His hands; who wakes you up each morning on time and with a sound mind; and who watches over every affair of your life because your life belongs to Him. Give the Lord all the praise, honor, and glory for His faithfulness towards you even when you are unfaithful. God wonderfully and perfectly created you for His glory; He has kept you thus far for a reason—to draw you closer unto Himself in relationship. Christ Jesus said, "Do not let your hearts be troubled. You believe in God; believe also in Me." (John 14:1 NIV). Your faith will come alive when you believe in the entirety of the Word of God. Christ said, "Most assuredly, I say to you, he who believes in Me, the works that I do he will do also; and greater works than these he will do, because I go to My Father." (John 14:12 NKJV). When a person truly believes in God, they act on what they believe and live according to the Word of God; when you believe, your faith comes alive in your actions. Again, Christ said, "He who believes in Me, as the Scripture has said, out of his heart will flow rivers of living water." (John 7:38 NKJV). When you believe in the Lord, out of you will flow His Holy Spirit that will lead you into all truth and into eternity. It is your act of obedience towards God and His Word that makes the difference in hopeless situations. Let us declare and proclaim God's Word to this dying world, God is looking for true believers all over the world that are ready to take His Word in obedience and walk in the power of His Holy Spirit. Whatever the Word of God says, It settles every doubt and fear. If the Word says, "...They will lay hands on the sick, and they will recover." (Mark 16: 17–18 NKJV). So shall it be. Then do just that; do not try to figure out how it is going to happen or question what if, or simply waver in unbelief and doubt. Just obey what the Word says because the authority comes from the Lord Jesus, since it is all about Him and never about us.

Again, my dear friend in Christ, if you do not know the Lord or have not surrendered to His lordship by accepting Him as your Lord and personal savior, and the repentance of your sins; I pray in the mighty name of Jesus Christ our Lord that His Holy Spirit will convict your heart unto repentance and salvation, that He takes His place in your heart for an eternal relationship. On the other hand, if you are a child of God, you know that you have become a new creation the day you gave your life to the Lord, the day you repented of all your sins and surrendered to His lordship over your life. You have become a new person through the precious blood of our Lord Jesus Christ, which has cleansed you from all unrighteousness through your faith in Him. Therefore, live in that authority of God that is freely given to us as believers; rule and reign over all things including principalities, powers, and spiritual wickedness in high places. Intentionally live and practice the ways of God, including purity, holiness, and integrity in all areas of your life and in your relationship with God, based in the truth that God has given us all things pertaining to life and godliness in His Word. *Only believe in the Lord Jesus Christ!*

LOVE THE LORD YOUR GOD

May God's divine Word continues to shape our lives and those around us with great signs and wonderous works to His glory, in His mighty name of Jesus. Amen! God is a good God, and His goodness is shown in our lives from the moment He wakes us up, to the time we fall asleep. The Lord does not treat us according to our deeds, but He showers us with His love, mercy, grace, and favor in every moment of our lives. No matter what is going on in our lives or in our world today, God is still who He is, He is still in control, and His Word is still the same. The Father is still sovereign over all things; no one or anything is above Him because heaven still rules. What God has said before, He is still saying now, and He will say forever. Even though we live in a changing world where nothing is stable, God's Word remains unchanging and unshakeable. The Word of God is eternal and will not be altered due to changes in our world. Whatever God has said in His Word is for our benefit; it is a lamp to our paths of righteousness, the light that our world desperately needs.

Let us go back to the Word in Deuteronomy 6, when the Lord God was laying down His rules for the Israelites, the people whom He had saved from the bondage of slavery in Egypt; the people whom He was taking to the land He had promised their forefather Abraham; and the people He was going to use to reveal Himself to as God almighty, and henceforth, reveal Himself to the rest of the world. God gave the Israelites His commands that they were to adhere to on their way to possess the land through His messenger Moses. These were commands they were to observe with reverential fear of God because the Lord God is a holy God, and His people must be holy. And obeying these commands, God said, will bring the people prosperity and long life. God's Word is His command for His children, and He expects His children to follow such in order to have a prosperous long life here on earth. As children of God, let us teach and encourage our loved ones the Word of the Lord, so that it will go well with us and with them in the Lord. "Hear O Israel: The LORD our God, the LORD is one! You shall love the LORD your God with all your heart, with all your soul, and with all your strength." (Deuteronomy 6:4–5 NKJV). Moses started by reminding the people of Israel that the Lord our God, the Lord is one. God is the same God that was in the beginning, the same God that spoke through the prophets, the same God that was in the burning bush, and the same God who was in the pillar of fire. He is the same God who created all things, who took on flesh as man to save humanity, the same who is the Holy Spirit in us, and who is coming again soon on that glorious day—Jesus Christ our Lord and God. *When you love the Lord Jesus, you are compelled by His Holy Spirit in you to please Him; His desire becomes your desire and His will your way of life.* You must love the Lord with no shadow of doubt and with all your heart, with all your soul, and with all your strength.

One's love for God is the first sign of His presence in them and it reveals their reverence for the Lord. Our love for the Lord Jesus is the foundation of a lifelong relationship, which started with Him first loving us with an everlasting love. Your lifestyle demonstrates God's love in you, your love for others, your worship, your prayer life, your time, and your relationship with Him. When you love the Lord, everything changes around you, in you and about you; it brings the Word of God alive in you. Love restores, heals, comforts, renews, and draws you closer to the presence of the almighty God. Be intentional my friends, as love itself is very intentional, and it brings forth actions of your faith based on the love of God in you. *The Christian faith is a 'love story,' it is about God's authentic love story (from Genesis to Revelation), revealing God's divine love for His people. Love is the centerpiece of God.* Let us love the Lord our God foolishly and do not hold back. Present your body as a living and holy sacrifice unto the Lord as your response to His love for you, and keep His Word in your heart as the Holy Spirit helps you to abide and obey Him in love. Wherever you go and in whatever you do, spread the love of the Father to others around you through your acts of love; let that fragrance of His presence in you be made known to all around you, to the praise of His glory. Seek the Lord earnestly while He may be found, and allow Him to reveal Himself in you through His Word and His Spirit; and as His Spirit starts to embrace you in love, in return, you also begin to fall in love with Him more and more.

God does not just want you to love Him, but to foolishly be in love with Him! The book of Romans shows us how God demonstrated His love for humanity, "But God demonstrates His own love toward us, in that while we were still sinners, Christ died for us." (Romans 5:8 NKJV). God is still loving us right now, and He will continue to love us forever: "For God so loved the world that He gave His only begotten Son, that whoever believes in Him should not perish but have everlasting life." (John 3:16 NKJV). God's love is so great that He does not want anyone to perish in Hell, but desire that all come to His saving knowledge and grace of His Son Jesus Christ. The Father longs for our love in response to His love for us; He wants us to be foolishly in love with Him like He is towards us; He wants us to have a *"Hallal"* kind of love (as referenced in the Hebrew language). *"Hallal"* in Hebrew means *"Praise"* and it means to: shine, boast, celebrate, commend, sing, be clear, laud, clamorously foolish, and joyfully excited about God. It implies the unashamed use of the voice in demonstration of what one thinks of God. Apostle Paul boldly declared his love for the gospel throughout his ministry. An example of such can be found in the book of Romans:

> For I am not ashamed of the gospel of Christ, for it is the power of God to salvation for everyone who believes... For in it the righteousness of God is revealed from faith to faith; as it is written, the just shall live by faith. (Romans 1:16–17 NKJV).

God expects us to be so in love with Him that we boast and rave to the extent that the world calls us *foolish*. No! we are not being foolish; we are just being obedient and loving our king and Lord. As the twenty-four elders around the throne in heaven declare continuously saying, "Thou art worthy O Lord, to receive glory and honor and power: for Thou hast created all things, and for thy pleasure they are and were created." (Revelation 4:11 KJV); so, we should also aspire with all sincerity to exalt the name of the Lord Jesus continuously in praise and worship and in all that we do. When we 'Hallal' in love, it must never be about us or others around us but all about the Lord, (the reason of our being) who deserves our every exhilaration. We cannot and must not see ourselves or even bother about how others see us when we are totally concerned and immersed in God's love. Our "Hallal" then becomes a continuous lifestyle of being in love and acting in love with *Love Himself (The Lord)*. It is amazing to see that the word "Hallal" is used in conjunction with the name of God "Jah," to form one of the most used words in the Bible for praise, i.e., "Hallelujah." Hallelujah has no language barriers, and it is used universally by both Christians and non-Christians. Hallelujah is used largely in the book of Psalms and it signifies the spontaneous outcry of anyone who is excited about God; it is a great love cry response to God's greatness, power, majesty, glory, holiness, and infinite love. According to the gospel of Matthew, Christ Jesus was asked to name the greatest commandment in the law, and His response was, "You shall love the LORD, your God, with all your heart, with all your soul, and with all your mind." (Matthew 22:37 NKJV). *Love is the greatest command, and it conquers all things— it overcomes every challenge. God is love and everyone that loves is indeed born of God and knows God; love is the foundation and heart of God Himself.* Hence, let us be encouraged to love one another. If we cannot love our fellow humans, how could we possibly love God whom we have never seen; our love for one another reflects the love of God in us.

As children of God, we have so many more reasons to love God more than anything this world could ever offer us. We have the presence of the living God living within us, His Holy Spirit. To genuinely express this quality of demonstrative love, we must refer to God's Word. To love God foolishly has its source in the degree to which our minds are meditating on God's Word; God's Word inspires us to *"Hallal."* It is the key to the expression of being proud and enthusiastically foolish about God. If we do not know the Word of God, we cannot do it, and we cannot expect others to do it. *Our substance of love is the Word of God in us.* In the book of Colossians, we are given the reason to experience joyful praise to the Lord: "Let the Word of Christ dwell in you richly in all wisdom, teaching, and admonishing one another in psalms and hymns and spiritual songs, singing with grace in your hearts to the Lord." (Colossians 3:16 NKJV). When the Word of God is dwelling in us richly, it will manifest through us as psalms and hymns and spiritual songs singing in our hearts to the Lord. We need to be dedicated to God's Word more than ever before as we draw closer to the coming of our Lord Jesus Christ. Let us *"Hallal"* and be foolishly in love with the Lord; and may His love compel us to declare His Word in every situation with confidence of who He is and what He has done because of the power in the spoken Word of God. May we also be doers of His Word by living the Word of the Lord through the power of the Holy Spirit in us.

LET US LIVE THE WORD OF GOD

Our duty as humans who have been wonderfully and perfectly created is to live according to the Word of God. Our actions and words must reflect whose we are and be in line with that of the Word of God. For example, here in the U.S., it is written on the dollar bill, 'In God we trust.' But the question for all Americans today is: *'Do we as a nation and people of God really trust in God? Are Americans living up to that statement or has this declaration simply become a cliché? Do Americans still love and trust the God who gave this land to their forefathers? Or do most trust in themselves now rather than trust in God?* These days fewer and fewer believers and non-believers have absolute regard for God or for the authority of the Scriptures. The future of this nation and the nations of the world depend on how its people relate to the revelation God has given in His Word. If God's children would keep the Word of God prominent in their lives, if they would meditate on the Word of God day and night, forsake their ways, return to the Lord in reverence and surrender, and if they would follow the precepts of the Lord; then, the Father will rejoice in heaven and return once more to His people with great reward. When God's divine name is being glorified here on earth as it is in heaven, the world will experience the manifestation of the power, knowledge, wisdom, and favor of God in the lives of His children. On the other hand, when God's children set aside the Word of the Lord and the relationship with their creator and choose to follow their own ways, this is a clear rejection of the knowledge and wisdom of God. The Word of God tells us that, "The fear of the LORD is the beginning of all wisdom, and knowledge of the Holy One is understanding." (Proverbs 9:10 NIV). *When you truly love the Lord with your entire being, and you know, reverence, and understand who He is, your actions will reflect your belief and faith in Him.* Hence, when one rejects the Word of the Lord, they simply reject the wisdom and knowledge of their creator. Consequently, when nations reject what God has already said in His Word, they have basically forsaken the wisdom that is available to them. The Word of God is readily available to all His children as it has always been from generation to generation. Thank God that the availability of the Word of God for the most part, is not the problem today nor has it ever been the problem in times past. The problem is that people have not embraced the Word of God as the manual or blueprint of life; people have rejected and turned away from the Word of the Lord and as a result they have no knowledge of the Father. *The wisdom of the nations is to hear the Word of the Lord and let that Word direct their course in life.*

There is a drifting from the Word or perhaps even a forsaking of the Word of the Lord; people are no longer turning to the Scriptures to connect with God. God's children should go back to the basics and let God rule and reign in their lives; let the Word of the living God come alive in God's children. In other words, God's Word should be manifested with the power of the Holy Spirit in the lives of God's people—*let us live the Word of God*. Let us live the Word of God by respecting the authority of the revelation in the Word. God's children need to change their attitude toward the Word of God; the Bible is a revelation of God from God, designed to show us the way of salvation, and to show us how to live a godly life here on earth and into eternity. God's Word is authoritative above all other ideas because it comes to us from the creator. Let us be mindful of the warnings of the Word according to apostle Paul in the book of Colossians, "Beware lest anyone cheat you through philosophy and empty deceit, according to the tradition of men, according to the basic principles of the world, and not according to Christ." (Colossians 2:8 NKJV). There are philosophies of this world that are asserting influence all around us; there are ways of viewing life that are contrary to God's will, and God's children are influenced by these philosophies and patterns of this world. Apostle Paul warns that we must watch out in order not to be deceived by those ideologies of people. As God's children, we cannot allow ourselves to be bought into a world system that does not acknowledge the principles of God. Today, in our world, the rule of life has become whatsoever feels right for individuals of this world system; people conduct their lives the way they want to live, instead of living the way God wants them to live. They have turned away from the Lord and come up with their own ways that will not stand. Hence, such are now under the judgement of God because there are boundaries established by God as to what is right and acceptable, versus what is wrong and not acceptable. Since God made all things and He owns it all, He is the one who decides what those boundaries are; and He has revealed those boundaries in His Word and the consequences for rebelling against His plan.

Friend, what God has said in His Word is still *true* today; He is the same yesterday, today, and forever. God does not change and neither does His complete truth that is rooted in His Word (Hebrew 13:8 NIV). If God's children think they can make up sets of rules to replace the limitations God has already revealed in His Word, they are miserably mistaken. It is a fatal mistake to simply ignore what God has told us to do and make up our own rules to follow in life. God's people have turned from the Lord's ways and come up with theirs; this has been the same sin from generation to generation, and we know that there is a consequence for sin—*death* (spiritual and then physical). We should endeavor to live our lives according to God's will; let us live the Word of our Father. God has revealed His plan in His Word that stands forever; and His Word is for our admonition and way to go. God's Word is firmly established in heaven; it is not up for debate. Christ Jesus said, "Heaven and earth will pass away; but My Words will never pass away." (Luke 21:33 NIV). All the things of this world that people fervently chase after instead of the creator will all pass away and perish; only one thing will remain, which is the Word of God.

Let us live the Word by meditating on the revelation God has given in His Word. Children of God should engage the Word with their minds; they are to read it, study it, ponder its meaning for their lives, and allow the Word to fill their thoughts through the power of the Holy Spirit in them. Children of God should always reflect on what God has said in His Word regarding what they are doing; they should always have God on their minds. We should endeavor to create special times when we can set aside other things and give more focus to our meditation of the Word, as well as our relationship with our creator, savior, and sustainer of our lives. It is not enough only on a Sunday mornings or Wednesday evenings to study and believe the Bible to be the inspired and authoritative Word of God. We must engage the Word in our daily routines on a regular basis so that we know what it says and apply it into our lives. The Word of God must be applied to our daily decisions; it must shape our worldview, determine how we think about and value things, and ultimately direct how we live our lives. The Word of God tells us that, "Man shall not live by bread alone, but by every word that proceeds from the mouth of God." (Matthew 4:4 NKJV). *Life is not sustained by material nutrition alone, but life is sustained by feeding upon the Word of God.* Our bodies need food to nourish and keep us alive, but our spirits (the very core of our being) need the Word of God to live on and live abundantly in the Lord, since we are spirit beings clothed in a body.

Wisdom of God is only complete when we have respect for His Word, and meditate on that Word; thereby, living according to the Word. In the actual practice of the Word, in doing what God has said to do, we become wise. "But be doers of the Word, and not hearers only, deceiving yourselves." (James 1:22 NKJV). So, let us abide in the Word, in the sense that we draw spiritual sustenance from it, and it directs our actions in life. In the gospel of John, Christ says, "My sheep hear My voice, and I know them, and they follow Me." (John 10:27 NKJV). Also, "But all who reject Me, and My message will be judged on the day of judgement by the truth I have spoken." (John 12:48 NLT). The very Word of God rejected by many these last days will be the judge on judgement day. Now exalt the Lord, our God through His never changing Word, in your everyday life; exalt the Lord of host according to His Word, for He is worthy of all glory, honor, and praise!

EXALT THE LORD OUR GOD

Father, in the name of Jesus Christ our Lord, we want to exalt You for all that You are, and for giving us another chance to draw closer to You this very moment. We exalt You for another privilege to turn from our wicked and selfish ways, and unto knowing You more. God almighty, be thou glorified in our hearts O Lord, and in our daily lives my Lord. For You have created all things in heaven, on earth, and under the earth in Your great power and mighty strength and for Your glory they are and were created. To whom shall we compare You O God or who is Your equal, O holy one? We bless Your mighty name! Your name is above every other name, above every problem, and at the mention of Your name, Lord Jesus, every situation shall bow. Father, you stretched out the heavens like a canopy and spread them out like a tent to live in. You are the everlasting God, the great I am, the ancient of days. Your kingdom is an everlasting kingdom, and Your dominion endures throughout all generations; be exalted O Lord! We praise Your holy name forever and ever, for there is none holy like You Lord; there is none besides You, and neither is there any rock like our God. You sit enthroned high and exalted between the cherubim, clothed in light and glory, and Your splendor fills the temple. Seated in Your presence, O Lord, are seraphim who never stop praising You saying: "Holy, holy, holy is the Lord almighty; the whole earth is full of the His glory." (Isaiah 6:3 NIV). Together with all the hosts of heaven, we fall before Your presence in adoration and awe of You, our Lord and redeemer. Amen!

The heavens declare Your glory, the skies, and all of creation proclaim the works of Your hand. They all show forth Your great and mighty power; Your power is over all other powers. You do not grow tired, and Your understanding no one can fathom. You give strength to the weary and increases the power of the weak; those who put their hope and trust in You Lord, shall be empowered and renewed in every way. You deserve our praise O sovereign God! You hold everything together and remains faithful to all Your creation; You open Your hands and satisfy every living creature with favor; we give You all the glory! May all Your creation bless and gratefully praise Your holy name forever and ever. You are good to all and Your mercies are over all Your works, and over the entirety of Your creation. Take all the glory, honor, and praise for You are God our creator, and You have loved us with an everlasting love. Thank You for calling us into Your presence; be exalted O God! Amen!

The Bible tells us to exalt the Lord our God and to worship Him whilst we have the time and breath of life (Psalms 99:5 NKJV). Let us worship the Lord with our all and all, for our God is a consuming fire, and He is worthy of our every praise. Praise and exalt God for His marvelous works and for His holy name:

> Praise the LORD! Praise God in His sanctuary; praise Him in His mighty firmament! Praise Him for His mighty acts, praise Him according to His excellent greatness! Praise Him with trumpet sound; praise Him with flute and harp! Praise Him with timbrel and dance; praise Him with stringed instruments and flutes! Praise Him with loud cymbals; praise Him with clashing cymbals! Let everything that has breath praise the LORD. Praise the Lord! (Psalms 150:1–6 NKJV).

Our bodies are the temple of God and God's Spirit resides in us, in our mortal bodies; therefore, we have every reason to exalt His name here on earth. Let us exalt the name of the living God who has given us a kingdom that cannot be shaken, and thus let us offer to God acceptable worship, with reverence, and awe of Him. True worship must be in spirit,—with the leadership of the Holy Spirit of God, and we must be engaged in it with our whole heart declaring that God is worthy of our reverence. Let us worship God and exalt His name based on the truth of His nature and character. Most importantly, Christ Jesus made us to understand that God alone deserves our worship and nothing else (Luke 4:8 NIV). People continue to worship all sorts of things today other than God, some worship their social groups, jobs, others their pastors, religious leaders, doctors, achievements, economic status, material things, and children. Anything that stops a person from worshipping the Lord their maker is an *idol* in their life; if that thing is more precious to you than God or His Word, then it is an idol and a sin. "You shall worship the LORD your God, and Him only you shall serve." (Luke 4:8 NKJV).

I believe that a time is coming when all of God's people shall fall at His feet and worship Him because His Words says so, "All nations whom You have made shall come and worship before You, O Lord, and shall glorify Your name." (Psalms 86:9 NKJV). John the revelator also confirmed this glorious day, when all of creation shall worship the Lord God almighty: "Then I heard every creature in heaven and on earth and under the earth and on the sea, and all that is in them, saying: "To Him who sits on the throne and to the Lamb be praise and honor and glory and power, FOREVER AND EVER!" (Revelation 5:13 NIV). The Lord is good, and His mercies endures to all generations; great and awesome are His deeds, and He is the Lord God, the almighty and the King of the nations! I appeal to you therefore, as children of God, that we intentionally and sincerely present our ways and entire being as a holy form of worship to the Lord, our God. Let worship and thanksgiving to the Lord God be in every aspect of our daily lives, as we imitate and draw strength from those who were before us in the faith. Let us use God's spoken Word to praise Him, for His Word is truth and powerful.

O Lord our God; we exalt and praise Your holy name, for You have done wonderful things, things planned long ago, faithful and sure (Isaiah 25:1 NIV). Let us extol the Lord in the congregation of the people and praise Him in the assembly of the elders (Psalms 107:32 NIV). Let us give thanks and make a joyful noise to the Lord for all that He has done. We should always be excited when we come before the Lord in praise and worship; it must not be a burden to serve the Lord, but a time of gladness and appreciation of hearts for His faithfulness, grace, and love towards us. David said, let us sing to the Lord a new song; let us sing to the Lord, all the earth; let us worship and bow down, let us kneel before the Lord, our maker; for He is our God, and His faithfulness is all around us each moment of our lives. Today, if you hear His voice, do not harden your heart or turn from His still quiet voice within you. Let God into your heart through Christ Jesus and start that life changing relationship with Him; you will never regret walking with the Lord. Let the light of Christ in you shine for all to see, and give glory to the Father.

LET YOUR LIGHT SHINE

We know and believe that Christ Jesus is the light of the world, the source of spiritual light to the world; and if we follow Him, we shall never walk in darkness (follow the wicked ways of this world), but we will have the light of life, which is Christ Jesus. Our world is full of darkness due to the wicked acts of people, because people have turned away from the ways of God and follow their own set of ways. Christ is that light that we need to guide our lifelong journey in order to be the people He has created us to be. As children of God, we have the full assurance of walking in the light of God even as we allow His Holy Spirit to lead and guide us in our daily lives. Just as Christ came as the light of the world, He also commands us to be lights too when He said:

> You are the light of the world. A city that is set on a hill cannot be hidden. Nor do they light a lamp and put it under a basket, but on a lampstand, and it gives light to all who are in the house. Let your light so shine before men, that they may see your good works and glorify your Father in heaven. (Matthew 5:14–16 NKJV).

May the light of Christ in you, even in this dark world, shine before others through your actions of faith—your good deeds, by encouraging one another, by praying for one another, by helping others, by spreading the good news of Christ to friends and family, by loving others, and by making a difference in the lives of others, to the glory of God the Father. God has delivered us from the kingdom of darkness and into His marvelous light, and this light is in us, who believe in Christ Jesus. If you are in Christ, you cannot hide that light because that light is Christ in you, and it cannot be hidden; the light in you is bound to shine for all to see and give glory to God.

Even though we still live in this dark world, and at one time we were in darkness through our sins; we are no longer of this world and its sinful desires because we have now come to the knowledge of the light. Hence forth, we live as children of light through the power of His Holy Spirit in us. So, my dear friends in the Lord, let your light shine in the darkest corners of this world, let it shine on the unsaved, let it shine on the homeless, let it shine on the most privileged and on the less privileged; let it shine on the helpless, those that have been torn apart by the pull factors of this world, and let your light shine in this crooked and twisted generation to the glory and praise of God. Fear not, for nothing will stand in the way of the light as Christ has overcome every force of the enemy, and He has won the victory. Let the light of Christ in us shine through every Word of God we declare in the mighty name of Jesus Christ, because there is power in the spoken Word of God!

The Lord Jesus Christ promised us that when we follow Him, we will never work in darkness, we will never follow the ways of sin, or live in a state of continually sinning, but we will repent of our sins and stay close to the light of the world. Also, when we follow Christ, we will reflect Him who is the light of life. The light in us is evidence to others of our faith, expressed by our good deeds, and through the power of the Holy Spirit at work in us.

We must be credible witnesses in this world; a witness that shows us to be faithful, God fearing, trustworthy, sincere, and honest in all that we do and speak. We should always be ready to give an account of the hope that we have in Christ, as mentioned in the Word: "But in your hearts revere Christ as Lord. Always be prepared to give an answer to everyone who asks you to give the reason for the hope that you have. But do this with gentleness and respect." (1 Peter 3:15 NIV). For the gospel of light that we have is not to be covered but to be made obvious for all to see and benefit from it; so that others too may come into the light of Christ Jesus our Lord.

Walk in the light of life by acting correctly and living openly for God's glory. Walking in the light is directly related to following Christ Jesus, living one's life in Him. Our lifestyle can be considered a *walk*. Walking in the light is also related to growth—it is taking steps toward maturity in Christ. "Light" in the Bible can be a metaphor for life, righteousness, or understanding. Walking in the light simply means, *growing in holiness and maturing in the faith as we follow Christ Jesus*. Walking in the light also means, we consider Christ Jesus as "The light" in this dark world, and we walk in that light by following His precepts, living in His power, and growing in His grace. Here are some examples in the Old Testament about walking in the light: "O House of Jacob, come and let us walk in the light of the LORD." (Isaiah 2:5 NKJV). "For you have delivered me from death and my feet from stumbling, that I may walk before God in the light of life." (Psalms 56:13 NIV). "Blessed are those who have learned to acclaim you, who walk in the light of your presence, LORD." (Psalms 89:15 NIV). "The people walking in darkness have seen a great light; on those living in the land of deep darkness a light has dawned." (Isaiah 9:2 NIV). As Christians, our responsibility is to live in the light (Christ Jesus) God has given us, speak the unchanging Word of God, speak what Christ Jesus says, and see it come to pass for His name's sake because of the power in His

Word. We give thanks and praise to the Lord for our existence and redemption through Christ our Lord. Amen!

BE THANKFUL TO GOD

The Lord God wants us to be thankful for everything that He has done, and everything that He continuously do in our lives. Thank God that you exist, thank Him that you have been redeemed from sin, thank the Lord that your debt is fully paid for your sins, and thank Him that the sentence of punishment for your sins is served completely at calvary. *It is done! The battle is fully won; all bondage of sickness, pain, disease, and disappointment from the enemy is broken and we are free like a bird. Hallelujah!* It is a miracle and privilege that we exist; God chose our existence to happen at an ordained time according to His plan and purpose. It really is a privilege to be alive today at such an exciting time as now, in such a dynamic and rapid changing world. God wants us to be aware of this fact, and to express our praise in every way to Him. The book of Psalms is a guide for praise and worship; it shows the psalmist's response to the faithfulness of God including the miracle of his existence. This appreciation is often associated to the lifting of our hands in worship. Our praise with hands lifted is a confession of praiseful thanks for creation, and it is one of the most powerful expressions of praise that exists. It is an acknowledgement that the Lord who made us, has brought us to this privileged place of being able to appreciate His handiwork in us. Next time you lift your hands in praise, thank Him for the fact that He wonderfully and perfectly created you. God not only wants us to appreciate the fact that He created us and not we ourselves, but also wants us to acknowledge the fact that we have been redeemed through Christ our Lord. "Oh, give thanks to the LORD, for He is good! For His mercy endures forever. Let the redeemed of the LORD say so, whom He has redeemed from the hand of the enemy." (Psalms 107:1–2 NKJV). The Lord did not only perform the miracle of creating us, but He also redeems us. The revelation of this Scripture gives fresh importance to praising God, who has redeemed us from the hand of the enemy that seeks to destroy us, that seeks to stop us from giving praise to God. The enemy seeks to steal our joy that comes from above, and seeks to stop us from worshipping the living God. It will undeniably take eternity to thank God for all that He has done for us including our deliverance and safekeeping. We truly have been delivered and we should not be ashamed of thanking the Lord Jesus and giving Him praise always for His loving kindness and faithfulness towards all His creation. God's faithfulness is upon us and His breath of life is in us.

Let us also remember that we have an obligation to first give thanks to God for who He is, for all that He has done for us, for all He has done through us, for all that He has done in others, and for all that He has done for the nations of this world. For the Bible says, "...Apart from Me you can do nothing." (John 15:5 NIV). One basic but important subject that I would like to remind you about is that of *ingratitude*. A simple definition of ingratitude is defined as "Lack of proper appreciation or thanks for something (such as a kind or helpful act): lack of gratitude" (Mariam Webster). Ingratitude is a basic sin that is overlooked by many, including children of God. The apostle Paul reminded us:

> Since what may be known about God is plain to them because God has made it plain to them. For since the creation of the world, God's invisible qualities—His eternal power and divine nature— have been clearly seen, being understood from what has been made, so that people are without excuse. For although they knew God, they neither glorified Him as God nor gave thanks to Him, but their thinking became futile, and their foolish hearts were darkened. (Romans 1:19–21 NIV).

It is apparent that humans have no excuse for rejecting Christ Jesus as Lord, since God has given to all humanity the opportunity to believe in Him. He has placed inside of us the choice to freely choose life or death through Christ Jesus. The sin of ingratitude nullifies this very important fact that God alone is worthy to receive glory and thanksgiving from all people. This fundamental truth is known to all, and all are without excuse. Therefore, we all must answer to Him who is the truth (Christ Jesus). *The ultimate sin of ingratitude is knowing that there is a God but attempting to live as if God does not exist. It is to live our lives without the one (God) who gave us the life and sustains it.*

Hence, to fully understand the reality of God's love, namely, salvation, we must be thankful to God. If we are not thankful, we have not fully grasped the reality of salvation. Salvation is not just to escape hell by repenting of your sins and accepting Christ as personal savior, but moreover, it is the appreciation of the privilege of enjoying fellowship with the Lord. It was God who chose to save us by His own will, and who predestined us to be conformed to the image of His Son. Thus, it is not right to live in God's kingdom without gratitude. The ramification of being saved is an ongoing process of acknowledging the change that God continuously effects in our lives. If we do not discover this ongoing process of change from the time of our salvation, then, there is nothing to be thankful for. A repentant heart must be a thankful heart (1 Timothy 1:12–15 NIV). Believing in your heart that Jesus Christ is the Son of God, who laid down His life to give you yours, is the basis of thanksgiving. *There is no true salvation and repentance outside of a thankful heart; salvation and thanksgiving are inseparable.* As we grow in God and receive greater revelation of what salvation means, our thankfulness will also grow. So, speak the Word of God with a thankful heart for what He has already done on the cross, which is a continual act. Remember, this world is not our home, we are just passing through; we came from glory and into glory we shall surely return one day!

THIS WORLD IS NOT OUR HOME

Why is it that one will never feel content with their worldly achievements in this journey of life, or sometimes you feel like you do not belong to this world? The reason is plain and simple— as children of God, we are no longer of this world, for we are heading for an eternal place in the Lord Himself. By faith, when Abraham was called by God to leave his home, his people, and familiar environment and to go to a foreign place, he obeyed. Even though he made his home in this foreign land, the Bible tells us that, Abraham and his descendants (Isaac and Jacob) lived there like strangers in tents; waiting expectantly and confidently because they were looking for an eternal heavenly place far above what this temporal world could offer them. Abraham was confident and focused on finding that everlasting building or city in God Himself; he wanted God Himself (to know Him more and forever dwell in His presence). Abraham was seeking a sure and solid foundation whose builder is God Himself (Christ Jesus, our Lord).

The reason why we do not feel fit into the pattern of this world, the reason why we just do not get satisfied no matter what we achieve in this life, is because we are desiring the *living bread of life. We are looking for an eternal home, an eternal satisfaction for our souls, which cannot be found in anything this world can ever offer us, but it can only be found in the Lord God Himself—in a relationship with Christ Jesus our Lord.* This world is indeed not our home, we are just passing through; we are like strangers in a foreign land. That hunger and thirst in your soul can never be satisfied; that emptiness in your soul can never be filled until you surrender to your creator and savior Jesus Christ. Once you are connected to your source of life (Christ), like an electric switch, your light will turn on; then you will discover your purpose in this journey of life, and you will realize your true potential and identity. God's desires become your desires because your focus converts eternally and heavenly. Like Abraham, may God become so real to us that the physical does not matter anymore. In other words, we understand that the spiritual realm of the kingdom of God is far greater, deeper, and more powerful than any other realm. As my dear husband John always says, *"When your mind is truly renewed, when you are truly born again of the Spirit of God, the way you view and do things will be completely different and changed from that of the world."* Meaning that, you have been changed from the inside out (saved indeed), and you become Christ like—in mind and in deeds.

Press on to lay hold of the Lord, as the apostle Paul mentioned in Philippians:

> Not that I have already obtained all this, or have arrived at my goal, but I press on to take hold of that for which Christ Jesus took hold of me. Brothers and sisters, I do not consider myself yet to have taken hold of it. But one thing I do: Forgetting what is behind and straining toward what is ahead. I press on toward the goal to win the prize for which God has called me heavenward in Christ Jesus. (Philippians 3:12–14 NIV).

Paul was not focusing on his past or earthly achievements, but his eyes were fully on Christ, who had given him a second chance in life for the glory of God. He understood the power, love, and compassion of God upon his life. Christ Jesus became real to him after his supernatural experience and transformation on his way to persecute God's people in Damascus. Let us press on to lay hold of that for which God has created us and called us to do according to His will. Let us prepare for that city (whose builder is God Himself), where the streets are made of gold, and where there will be no more sickness, pain, nor dying. Paul's life was transformed and set apart for God's glory and honor; he became a new creation in Christ Jesus for a particular work. Paul's focus was shifted, becoming heavenward, just as Abraham's. Likewise, let our focus be heavenward, and no more of the fleeting desires of our flesh or of this wicked world. Let us desire more of the kingdom of God, desire more for the city of God, seek to know Him more and more, and long for the manifestation of His power and honor through His Word. Let us put Him first because He is the *first!*

PUT GOD FIRST

The Holy Spirit impressed upon me the importance of putting God first in everything that we do. Our Lord Jesus preached that the purpose of human life is to form a special relationship with God. In essence, we are to love, reverence, and adore God; we are to put Him first in everything. It is that simple. Yes, it is that simple. But based on human strength alone, this seems impossible to carryout. Christ Jesus says that to love God means to place Him first in our lives (hearts, bodies, souls, spirits, and minds).

> You shall love the LORD your God with all your heart, with all your soul, and with all your strength. And these words which I command you today shall be in your heart. You shall teach them diligently to your children and shall talk of them when you sit in your house, when you walk by the way, when you lie down, and when you rise up. You shall bind them as a sign on your hand, and they shall be as frontlets between your eyes. You shall write them on the doorposts of your house and on your gates. (Deuteronomy 6:5–9 NKJV).

We are commanded to put God first in everything we do; but what does it really mean to put God first? The Bible helps us to understand that virtually no one has really understood what it means to put God first in everything, nor how to accomplish such a task. But thank God, the way was finally revealed when Christ was on earth. He set Himself as an example of one who puts God first. Christ's lifestyle embodied what it meant to have a spiritual relationship with God. He said, "If anyone serves Me, let him follow Me..." (John 12:26 NKJV). The true believer would live his or her life exactly as Christ did—in relationship with the Father. Jesus explained this to His disciples saying, "If you keep My commandments, you will abide in My love, just as I have kept My Father's commandments and abide in His love." (John 15:10 NKJV). God's commandments reveal what God thinks, and how He looks at things; His commandments were fully manifested through the life of Christ Jesus. *It is only through Christ Jesus that we can fully understand the mind of God, the acts of God, the will of God, and the love of God for humanity.* The Holy Spirit within the believer reveals the mind of God to them; He discloses the things that God has prepared for those who love and trust Him, and who are called according to His purpose.

God has never dealt with humanity directly. In fact, the Bible tells us that the Ten Commandments, for example, were delivered by the Word—the Lord Jesus. The Word became flesh and dwelt amongst us; it is always Christ Jesus (in various offices throughout human history), who is revealing what the Father's commandments are through His Spirit. Christ is the *only* way, the truth, and the life. The Lord Jesus reiterated these words, "... Behold, I have come—in the volume of the book it is written of Me—to do Your will, O God." (Hebrews 10:7 NKJV). The Lord Jesus came to reveal the Father once more, and to make Him glorious and honorable; He showed that God's Word is the foundation of a loving relationship between human beings and God. Christ made the relationship clear by demonstrating it through His own living example. Henceforth, let us endeavor to follow God in Christ's footsteps; let us follow His ways and let His ways become our ways, His mind becomes our mind and His thoughts our thoughts through the help of His Spirit in us. Let us allow Christ to rule over our lives by putting Him at the center of everything that we do, and let us love others with the love of Christ in us because God is Love. When we put God first in our lives, we give Him the permission to have His way in our lives; we become more like Him, and He changes us for the better. We start to act like Christ, talk like Him, and love the way He Loves. Seek God first, put Him first in everything that you do, read His Word, and obey His commandments. Know Him more and more each day by seeking Him through His Word, through prayer and fellowship with Him, and through meditation upon His faithfulness. Pray continually to the Lord because only His kingdom, power, and glory are for ever and ever. He is a loving God, a faithful friend, and a good Father; so, seek after His heart by putting Him first in every area of your life. And His peace which surpasses all human knowledge and wisdom will guide and keep your heart and mind always through the power of His Holy Spirit. Amen!

LIVE A LIFE WORTHY OF THE LORD

Paul reminds the Colossians and Philippians churches of their responsibility to conduct themselves in a manner worthy of the gospel of Christ (Philippians 1:27 NIV). To be worthy of something requires much more than we could think and imagine—*we have a responsibility to it.* We have a responsibility as believers to live our lives worthy of the gospel. The English root word for "Worthy" is "Worth," meaning, how much something cost; the value of something. Merriam-Webster defines "Worthy" as good and deserving respect, praise, or attention, having worth or excellence. We should walk in a way that shows the extreme importance or extreme value of the gospel of Christ in our lives. Our lifestyle must reflect whom we have believed. The Word tells us in 1 Corinthians 15:2–4 that, as recipients of the gospel, we must hold fast and keep firmly what we have received and by which we have been saved. In this context, the Philippian church, was not walking worthily of the gospel due to persecution. They were under immense pressure to compromise their beliefs and their lifestyle. The same is true for us today. We are always being tempted to walk in an unworthy fashion by the devil, by our flesh, and by forces of this world. Nevertheless, as children born of the Spirit of God, we must endeavor to always demonstrate the extreme worth of the gospel; we must have the mind of Christ Jesus and walk in His way and truth with all confidence and pride. In the same manner, apostle Paul also prayed continually to God for the Colossian church. He asked God to fill them with the knowledge of His will through all the wisdom and understanding that the Spirit gives, so that they may live a life worthy of the Lord and that which is pleasing in His sight; a life that bears fruits in every good work. Fruits that will last by growing in the knowledge of God, being strengthened with all power according to God's glorious might. So that they might have great endurance, patience, and continually give joyful thanks to the Father, who has qualified them to share in the inheritance of His people. Likewise, the church should conduct themselves to a manner worthy of the Lord's sacrifice for us. For He has rescued us from the power of darkness and brought us into the kingdom of the Son He loves, in whom we have redemption and the forgiveness of sins (Colossians 1:9–14 NIV). Hallelujah, glory to God, and blessed be the name of the living God!

Every believer must endeavor to live a life worthy of the Lord; a lifestyle that reflects our Lord (in faith and in action), one that pleases Him in every way. Every child of God should conduct themselves to that of the image of Christ Jesus; having a mindset of Christ because even though we are still in this world, yet we are not of its patterns and ways. We do not act like that of the world, rather Christ must be reflected in all areas of our lives. Let the person next to you, your colleague, or that loved one, see the light of Christ in you by your fruits—your *actions of faith. Be that fragrance that is greatly needed in these dark days!* Now is the time to seek the Lord; tomorrow may be too late, and tomorrow is *never* guaranteed. Let us endeavor to reach out to God by showing forth His love in us to others, seeking Him, and calling on Him while we can. Christ first loved us, and His love compels us to also walk in love.

> Seek the LORD while he may be found; call on Him while He is near. Let the wicked forsake their ways and the unrighteous their thoughts. Let them turn to the LORD, and He will have mercy on them, and to our God, for He will freely pardon. "For My thoughts are not your thoughts, neither are your ways My ways," declares the LORD. "As the heavens are higher than the earth, so are My ways higher than your ways and My thoughts than your thoughts." (Isaiah 55:6–9 NIV).

God's grace is abundant and free for everyone; His mercy is calling us because His ways are always the best for us. The Lord is inviting us to come and enjoy His grace while it is near. The prophet Isaiah reminds us about God's gracious invitation and the importance for us not to ignore it. *God's grace is free and unlimited, but humans' time is limited; therefore, we do not have time to waste.* We do not have time to start procrastinating the calling of God upon our lives. The Lord Jesus is calling all people to humble themselves and seek Him, pray, turn from their wicked ways and call on Him while He is near. We must do our part; we have a responsibility and a duty to turn to the Lord and worship Him. *Now is the time!*

The Word of God reminds us, "For whosoever shall call upon the name of the Lord shall be saved." (Romans 10:13 KJV). All we must do is, to call on the name of the Lord Jesus, to be saved.

We are without excuse! *Call on Him while all is going well with you (when you are in good health, with sound mind, energetic, full of life, favored, and blessed); call on Him while you can, call on Him when you do not feel like it, and always call on Him.* Sooner rather than later; it may be too late as we have no control over our lives. Endeavor to know the Lord while you have the time and opportunity. Now is the appointed time—*right now, this very moment.* Do not turn it off; do not deny it! You may well be wondering what it means to 'Seek the Lord.' To seek the Lord means: call on Him, turn from our wicked ways and thoughts, depend on God for guidance, rely on Him rather than on our own human understanding. If we earnestly seek after the living God, seek after His heart with every fiber of our being, we will certainly find Him being a merciful and loving Father. "Ask, and it will be given to you; seek, and you will find; knock, and the door will be opened to you." (Matthew 7:7 NKJV). God is always near us; He is the reason why we are alive right now. He woke us up this morning right on time. We see His glory and goodness in all of creation. The Bible tells us, "The Lord is near to all who call on Him, to all who call in truth." (Psalms 145:18 NIV). We should seek God because we need to know His plans for our lives, since His plans are better than ours. God's plans for our lives are worth finding and knowing because only His plans will bring us to an expected end of everlasting life, joy, and peace. This starts through our worship and adoration of all that He is, and all that He has done. Come now let us exalt the king of glory!

O Lord our God, how excellent is Your name in all the earth! Father, we join the hosts of heaven in declaring that Thou art worthy O Lord, to receive all glory, honor, and power, for Thou has created all things and for Thy pleasure they are and were created. Thank You Father for giving us the privilege to serve you as Lord and God of all, through our obedience to Your will and purpose for each of us. May You reveal Yourself more and more to our friends all over the world. Father, please continue to have Your way in the lives of Your people through the power of Your Holy Spirit, that same Spirit that raised our Lord Jesus from the grave. May their lives never be the same as they earnestly seek Your presence, in reverence and awe. Glorify Your name in every area of our lives, so that all eyes will see and know that the Lord has done it. And now, may the Lord set you free, my dear friend, from every pull factor of this life, so that you may be the man or woman the Lord has created you to be for His glory and praise; may your desires be in line with that of the Father's as you seek His eternal kingdom, knowing fully well that this world is not your home, in Jesus' mighty name. Amen!

7

THE PROMISED HOLY SPIRIT

T he subject of the Holy Spirit is fundamental, and every child of God must understand it thoroughly with God's help because there is *no Christianity without the Holy Spirit.* Christianity was birthed through the Holy Spirit on the Day of Pentecost; hence Christianity without the Holy Spirit is dead Christianity. There is absolutely *no true Christianity without the leadership of the person of the Holy Spirit.* This is because, God is a Spirit, and His worshippers *must* worship Him in *Spirit.* Most Christians of today shy away from mentioning the Holy Spirit. Could this shyness be due to lack of knowledge about who He truly is, His role in the church, or role in the life of the believer; or could this shyness simply be *denial* since we are living in the perilous times as mentioned by our Lord Jesus and the apostle Paul? Apostle Paul brought to our attention regarding the last days:

> But know this, that in the last days perilous times
> will come: For men will be lovers of themselves,
> lovers of money, boastful, proud, blasphemers,
> disobedient to parents, unthankful, unholy,

unloving, unforgiving, slanderers, without self-control, brutal, despisers of good, traitors, headstrong, haughty, lovers of pleasure rather than lovers of God, having a form of godliness but denying its power. And from such people turn away! (2 Timothy 3:1–5 NKJV).

Sadly enough, my dear friends, this is our present world in which we live in. The Holy Spirit is talked about among believers or church folks, but His relationship, leadership, and power are denied. Without a relationship, the leadership, and power of the Holy Spirit, the gathering of so-called Christians become mere religion and business run by man's ideas and programs in the name of God. The Holy spirit is always disregarded in most Christian gatherings, and Christ Jesus clearly talked about it saying:

If you love Me, keep My commandments. And I will pray to the Father, and He will give you another Helper, that He may abide with you forever—the Spirit of truth, whom the world cannot receive, because it neither sees Him nor knows Him; but you know Him, for He dwells with you and will be in you. I will not leave you orphans; I will come to you. (John 14:15–18 NKJV).

The world and most so-called believers cannot accept the leadership of the Holy Spirit because they neither see nor know Him; but true believers that are born of the Spirit of God know Him because He dwells in them and is always with them. Just as the body without breath (life) is dead, and faith without works (actions) is dead; likewise, *Christianity without the Holy Spirit is a religion and a business, and therefore dead without the power and presence of God.* Without the Holy Spirit, our worship becomes a form of religious acts of business with no power to glorify the Father. Let us go back to the beginning of Christianity. The early church was built upon the revelation and leadership of the Holy Spirit, which started on the day of Pentecost. The leadership of the Spirit of God is the standard God has set for His children, and it still stands even today; we are still in the dispensation of the Holy Spirit, still in the era of the day of Pentecost. The promised coming of the Holy Spirit was prophesied even before the birth of Christ, around 609 B.C., by the prophet Joel saying:

> And afterward, I will pour out My Spirit on all people. Your sons and daughters will prophesy, your old men will dream dreams, your young men will see visions. Even on My servants, both men and women, I will pour out My Spirit in those days. (Joel 2:28–29 NIV).

God came back to His people, this time not in the flesh but in the form of the Holy Spirit. Christ promised in His Word that, He will never leave us nor forsake us, and that He will always be with us even to the very end. Also, Christ promised that He will not leave us like orphans but will come back unto us (John 14:18 NIV). This promised gift from God that took over 609 years was manifested upon the apostles on that glorious day of Pentecost. Christ came back to His people and He lives with us and in us forever, as promised. Yes, the Word of the Lord stands forever!

Here are some key questions we need to ponder upon when we talk about the Holy Spirit: Why did our Lord Jesus not start His ministry until He was baptized with the Holy Spirit, and why He needed the Holy Spirit to survive as a man here on earth? Or why did Christ tell His apostles to wait in Jerusalem until they were baptized with the Holy Spirit before stepping out to spread the good news of the gospel? Again, why was the baptism of the Holy Spirit needed for the early Christians after they had believed in the Lord Jesus? The one and only reason is that *there is no Christianity without the Holy Spirit, there is no Christianity without Christ, nor a worship of God without the Spirit of God;* it will only be *'antichrist or not of Christ.'* The presence of the Holy Spirit is the presence of God Himself because God is a Spirit, and His children must be born of the Spirit in order to enter the kingdom of God. Without the presence of the Holy Spirit in the lives of believers, in the gathering of God's people, there will be no revelation from God nor His power to do the things that only He can do in us; we can do *nothing* without the Holy Spirit. The presence of the Lord is not manifested in the gatherings of most believers today because *the leadership of the Holy Spirit has been substituted with human ideologies, programs, and rules.* The Holy Spirit is the head of God's people, and without Him there is no true worship of God. The prophets needed the presence of the Holy Spirit, so did our Lord Jesus, in order to survive and do all that He had to do in the flesh. The disciples also needed the Holy Spirit to lead and empower them for the great commission of spreading the good news of the gospel of Christ. Likewise, we (children of God) need the presence of the Holy Spirit in our everyday lives, in our churches, in our prayers, and in our walk with the Lord. We need the Holy Spirit especially in these perilous times, so that we will be able to stand against the evil spirits of the times through the Word of God. Those without the Spirit and the true Word of God are not of the Father and do not love Him nor love His Word. And since they are not of the Spirit of God, they cannot submit nor please Him, they are hostile to God, and the things of God because they spiritually separated from the Lord (spiritually dead). When you are born of the Spirit of God, you do mind (pay close attention to) the things of the Spirit as you work to always please the Lord; His desire becomes your desire.

We can never understand the deep things of God without the Spirit of God, nor can we worship the Father without His Spirit. Christians must receive or be filled with the Holy Spirit;

it is the Holy Spirit that seals us as children of God after we have received Christ as our savior. The Spirit then comes and makes His dwelling in us and remains with us forever as we stay steadfast in Him. You need the power and presence of the Holy Spirit in you and at work in you in order to live a successful Christian life—a life that is pleasing to the Father. *The presence of the Holy Spirit in a true Christian breaks every bondage.* We cannot serve God or have a relationship with the Lord Jesus without His Holy Spirit; it is the Holy Spirit that empowers us to do the things that God has called us to do; and without His leadership and power, we cannot do anything that will bring God the glory.

Moreover, the Holy Spirit is our all and in all—without Him nothing would have been possible behind everything pertaining to life and godliness. It is only through the Holy Spirit that we can produce fruits that will last. He was in the beginning, in every miracle that was ever performed by the prophets of God and even by Christ Jesus our Lord; nothing was done, and is done, without the presence of the Holy Spirit. Christ survived on earth because of the presence of the Holy Spirit with Him and at work in Him. If Christ needed the Holy Spirit in order to fulfill His mission on earth, what about us, or the church as a whole? Christ understood the importance of the Holy Spirit, which was why He warned His disciples to wait in Jerusalem for Him before stepping out into the world to witness the good news of salvation. And we understand that *when the apostles received the Holy Spirit, they were filled with supernatural power, boldness, love, and unity while preaching the gospel of Jesus Christ.* The original blessing, authority, and dominion given to humans by the Father at the time of creation were restored. God's authority was restored as the apostles ruled and subdued once more over every living creature upon the face of the earth; everything they declared and did was confirmed and achieved with miraculous signs and wonders. Nothing could stop them whatsoever; and every barrier was removed by the wonder working power of the Holy Spirit. For example, the apostles spoke the Word of God in the different languages of the people that were present as the Spirit gave them utterances. *The presence of the Holy Spirit in a believer is like a blaze of fire; He consumes, taking over the individual completely, as He makes him/her into a new creation, born of the Spirit of God.* Without the Holy Spirit in you, you will easily burnout and quit; but He gives us the strength, understanding, knowledge, and revelation in every step along this lifelong journey in Him. He is our source and our *all* and in *all*. Just as every living creature is dependent upon water and food for survival, so is a person's dependence upon the Holy Spirit. We need the Holy Spirit, the 'living water' to survive spiritually, or else we will also die (spiritually). We need the presence of the Holy Spirit in us like we need our next breath; He is our next breath, and makes it worth living. When the Holy Spirit comes into a person's life, He will renew, realign, refresh, refurnish, and restore that life to the glory of God the Father. Let us now go deeper in finding out who the Holy Spirit is, and define His mission in the lives of the children of God.

WHO IS THE HOLY SPIRIT AND WHY DID HE COME?

Some Christians may talk about the Holy Spirit, have heard, or read about Him, but deny and reject Him in every way possible. But "Who is the Holy Spirit?" Firstly, please understand the fact that the *Holy Spirit is not a thing, nor an emotion, or feeling; neither is He a dove or a floating power, as many people may have perceived.* The Bible tells us in John 16:13–14 that, the Holy Spirit is a *"Person" since* Christ refers to Him as *"He."* This clearly indicates that He is a person, meaning that He has the characteristics of a person—can choose, speaks, with feelings of the heart, can reason, and think etc. Thus, as a person, the Holy Spirit lives in a physical body of a true Christian, born of the Spirit of God. Without these characteristics of a person, the physical body is said to be dead;

that is why a body is declared dead because the spirit and the soul that hosted in that person's body departs or is no more. The person of the Holy Spirit has a mental faculty that can choose, speak, love, be grieved, vexed, be insulted, and be denied (Acts 20:28; 1 Corinthians 12:11; Hebrews 10:29; Ephesians 4:30; Romans 15:30 NIV). The Holy Spirit has all the attributes of a person, and He lives in those who believe in the Lord Jesus Christ, and who welcome Him into their lives; He then seals and approves them as children of God.

The Holy Spirit is not only a person, but the Father coming once more to His people in the form of the Spirit. God started His plan of love by revealing Himself to His people in different forms. *He is the same and only God, manifesting in different forms because He is "The I am"* (Exodus 3:14; John 6:35; 8:12; 10:7; 10:11; 11:25–26; 14:6 & 15:1 NKJV). During the Old Testament era, known as God the Father dispensation, the Father spoke directly to His prophets as a way of revealing Himself. In the New Testament, God comes in the flesh—in the form of a Son through Jesus Christ, born through the power of the Holy Spirit, to fulfill what God had planned earlier, which is the salvation of all humanity. Before Christ was taken into heaven, He reassured His disciples that He will not leave them as orphans but will come back through the Holy Spirit, whom the Father will send to be with them, and in them. When the Lord Jesus ascended back to the Father, the Holy Spirit was released by the Father as promised on the day of Pentecost, and He remains with us and in us that believe in the Lord Jesus, forever. The Holy Spirit is the comforter, the advocate, the counselor, the helper, the intercessor, the strengthener, the Spirit of truth, the teacher, the head of the church, the fulfiller of God's Word, the revelator (John 14:15–26; John 15:26; Acts 20:28; Revelation 2:7; 1 Corinthians 2:9–11 NIV). The Holy Spirit is the giver of life because every spoken Word of God is full of Spirit and life. We are living in God the Holy Spirit dispensation. He is the same Spirit that raised Jesus from the dead, that performed all the mighty works of God in both the Old and New Testament era, and the same that was at work in the disciples from the day of Pentecost. It is the same Holy Spirit that resides in you and me from the moment we accept the Lord Jesus as our savior and invites His Spirit into our hearts; He comes in and is ready to work with us if we allow Him to. "Now it is God who makes both us and you stand firm in Christ. He anointed us, set His seal of ownership on us, and put His Spirit in our hearts as a deposit, guaranteeing what is to come." (2 Corinthians1:21–22 NIV).

God gave the Holy Spirit to be with us, to comfort, counsel, teach, and to guide us in every area of our lives because of the Father's love for us. Do we deserve this love? Certainly not, but He has loved us with an everlasting love as a Father through Christ Jesus our Lord. The Holy Spirit, just like God's grace of salvation, is also a gift from God when we believe in His Son Jesus Christ as the sacrificial atonement for sin. We understand that God's grace is not something that we deserve but is an unmerited favor of God, that is not of our own effort or works. We are not saved because of our good works but through the grace of God that comes through faith in Christ Jesus. Nevertheless, our good works are a result of our faith in Christ and His Word, since faith without good works is no faith at all. Christ, during His ministry, performed great works as a result of His faith and love; the Bible tells us that everywhere He went He was doing good. Therefore, as children of God, we ought to do good everywhere we go, and in whatever we do; so that our Father may be glorified in heaven.

The Holy Spirit is the kingdom of God on earth with us and in us. He gives us the revelation, knowledge, and understanding of the things of God, especially to those, who love and trust in Him. The Holy Spirit is the one that convicts our hearts, and reveals Christ Jesus to us; He not only reveals Christ Jesus, but also the deep things of God to us, hence glorifying the Father through the Son. He is the fulfiller of God's Word, and He brings to pass every word and promise of God in the mighty name of Jesus. With the Lord Jesus now seated with the Father in heaven, the Holy Spirit is here on earth as promised by the Lord; so greater things shall we do in Him and through Him, to the glory of God. Friends, if you do not have the Holy Spirit and the Lord Jesus in your life, just ask Him today, right now, this very moment; ask Him to come into your heart and be your Lord and savior, and let Him have His way in you from now on. Allow the Holy Spirit to live and work fully in you to the glory of God; ask Him to take full pre-eminence in you for His name's sake. The apostle Paul has given us that relief by saying, "What we have received is not the spirit of the world, but the Spirit who is from God, so that we may understand what God has freely given us." (1 Corinthians 2:12 NIV). Without the presence of the Holy Spirit in the believer, the things of God can never be understood; it is the Spirit Himself that gives us the understanding and revelation of the things of God and of His Word. He reveals to the children of God those things that God has freely given to us that love Him; the Holy Spirit also reveals even things of the Father that are yet to come to His own. As it is written, "Eye has not seen, nor ear heard, nor have entered into the heart of man the things which God has prepared for those who love Him. But God has revealed them to us through His Spirit. For the Spirit searches all things, yes, the deep things of God." (1 Corinthians 2:9–10 NKJV). The Holy Spirit will receive from the Lord Jesus and make it known to us because He is here to *glorify* the Lord Jesus Christ.

Since the Holy Spirit comes as a gift to the believer and the church after we have received the Lord Jesus Christ, He will remain with us forever. He is the greatest gift to the children of God, just as Christ is the greatest sacrifice and love ever given for humanity; and when the Father gives His Holy Spirit, it is for His work and glory. When the gift of the Holy Spirit comes upon a person, it is not for them or about them, but it is for God's service and His glory. It is the Spirit that helps us to put to death the misdeeds of the body, He helps us in our weaknesses as He intercedes on our behalf, and leads us into paths of righteousness for His name's sake. Those that are not of Christ and live according to the flesh, do have their minds set on what the flesh desires, and such minds are hostile to God and the things of God; they are separated from God and His kingdom, and hence cannot do the things of God, nor submit or please the Father. However, the righteous are not so, for those who have Christ, those who are true children of God, live in accordance with the Spirit of God and have their minds set on what the Spirit desires, which leads to abundant life, joy, and peace in Him. The Holy Spirit is the person that calls or selects individuals to Himself, and to do His will. The children of God should be in the Spirit of Christ and not in the flesh of their minds, in order not to usurp the name of the Lord. The Holy Spirit must be the head and leader of the church since it is all about Him and never about you or me. So then, where is boasting and failure when you are fully in Christ? The Holy Spirit comes in the name of Christ Jesus to glorify Him regarding what He has done; He teaches us all things and reminds us of everything that Christ has said and done in His Word. It is the Holy Spirit that guides us into all truth and shows us the right path to go. The Holy Spirit is our counselor, our helper, our intercessor, our advocate, our strengthener, our standby, and our comforter. It is never based on human effort or leadership but the Holy Spirit's; His leadership is the blueprint for the children of God because without Him, there is no true worship, no true relationship, or true church. *Without the Holy Spirit, we can do or be absolutely nothing.*

The Holy Spirit came to be in companionship and have a relationship with us. He is that still quiet voice within the believer that convicts our hearts of the truth, God's love, and His saving grace towards us. He is the one that *convicts* the heart of sin, righteousness, and judgment; He proves the world of sin because people do not believe in Him. The Holy Spirit came to give power and boldness to the body of Christ—the true church, the true children of God. The Holy Spirit is the one that empowers and prepares us for the second coming of our Lord Jesus Christ (known as '*The Rapture*,' which is to come). We cannot reach the Father nor the Son without the Holy Spirit, we only have access through Him (Ephesians 2:18 NIV). The Holy Spirit, the Father, or the Son, are all the *one and same God*; one God manifested in different forms or offices as we have already mentioned. Christ confirmed this mystery by saying:

> Have I been with you so long, and yet you have not known Me, Philip? He who has seen Me has seen the Father; so how can you say, 'Show us the Father'? Do you not believe that I am in the Father, and the Father in Me? The words that I speak to you I do not speak on My own authority; but the Father who dwells in Me does the works. Believe Me that I am in the Father and the Father in Me, or else believe Me for the sake of the works themselves. (John 14:9–11 NKJV).

The Holy Spirit is God; He is Christ in the form of the Spirit, and He brings every Word of God, every spoken Word of Christ into existence. Declare that promise of God concerning your situation and see the power of the Holy Spirit bring it to pass through your faith in Him. Yes, my dear friends, your unwavering faith in the Lord Jesus Christ will make you whole, it will change impossibility into possibility, and bring back life into that deadly situation.

The Holy Spirit came to give us peace because Jesus Christ has overcome the world through His shed blood and resurrection. He said: "I have told you these things, so that in Me you may have peace. In this world you will have trouble. But take heart! I have overcome the world." (John 16:33 NIV). Christ is our peace in this troubled world, and we must believe, trust, and lean on Him, on His Word, and on His Spirit; we must delight in Him, and commit our ways unto Him through His Holy Spirit, whom He has freely given unto us, to guide and be with us forever. Even though we cannot see the Holy Spirit physically, nevertheless, we who are born of the Spirit of God know that He is in us and always with us. Like the air we breathe, we cannot see it, but does that mean it is not real? God exists, and so is His Holy Spirit on earth; He is a rewarder to those that diligently seek and accept Him. We cannot worship God if we do not believe in His existence or His Word. Every Word the Father has spoken is trustworthy, and it stands then, now, and forever. God moves through His Spirit in His obedient and humble children; He operates through His Spirit and faith in us. *We need the presence of the Holy Spirit in our homes, in our businesses, in our worship, in our churches, in our relationships, in our schools, in our workplaces, and certainly in every area of our lives.* Without the help of the Holy Spirit, your labor in the Lord is in vain because the presence of the Holy Spirit is the presence of Christ in you. He is the one that orders the steps of the righteous and makes their way perfect. The Holy Spirit is the light for your path and a lamp unto your feet. He is the reason of the church and the faith—the Holy Spirit is Christ Jesus; He is the Father, the almighty, and creator of all things in heaven, on earth, and under the earth.

The Holy Spirit is so important in the kingdom of God that sinning against Him will never be forgiven, according to the Word of God. It is the only sin that cannot be forgiven (Titus 1:16; 2 Timothy 3:5 NIV). Sinning against or grieving the Holy Spirit, simply means unbelief; it is denying or rejecting His authority, His presence, His power, and even His existence. The apostle Paul in Ephesians 4:30 tells us that, we should not grieve the Holy Spirit as it hinders a godly lifestyle. *A person cannot say they are a Christian but do not live by the Spirit or do what the Word says. One must be a Christian of the Spirit of Christ and not of the flesh (usurping the name of Christ in vain and living lives that are contrary to the Spirit of God).* Sadly enough, in these End Times, people declare that they are Christians because they simply subscribe in theory to the qualities of Christ Jesus—that is, to the fact that Jesus is the Son of God, born of a virgin, crucified, died, rose again, and savior of humanity; while living their lives contrary to the Word of God and denying the deity and power of His Spirit. True Christians are filled with the Spirit of God, led and live by the same Spirit, and have the signs and gifts of the Spirit in their midst. Your fruit, which the Spirit of God in you accomplishes must be that of Christ, and it springs forth from the love of the Father, which is in Christ Jesus our Lord. Love must be the centerpiece of our relationship with the Lord because God is love; hence those that are of Christ live in His love through the power of the Holy Spirit in them. When you invite the Spirit of God into your life and allow Him to take full control, you will find abundant life and receive favor and peace from the Lord; in the person of the Holy Spirit there is life, and that life is the light of all men (Proverbs 8:35 NIV). *Again, I say, it is impossible to live a successful Christian life without the presence of the Holy Spirit; it is the Holy Spirit in us, with us, and through us that we can produce fruits that will endure into eternity. His presence is Christ in that individual.*

The Holy Spirit enables us as we live and walk in the Lord. He strengthens us in our weaknesses; when we are weak, then we are strong because His strength becomes our strength, as He perfects us. Only then can we boast in our weaknesses in order that we may be strengthen for His glory. The Holy Spirit breaks every chain of the devil in our lives, and sets us free from bondages of sin, sicknesses, diseases, hopelessness, faithlessness, unworthiness, ungodliness, and so on and so forth. He is our weapon and strength to destroy every works of the enemy.

> For the weapons of our warfare are not carnal but
> mighty in God for pulling down of strongholds,

casting down arguments and every high thing
that exalts itself against the knowledge of God,
bringing every thought into captivity to the
obedience of Christ, and being ready to punish
all disobedience when your obedience is fulfilled.
(2 Corinthians 10:4–6 NKJV).

The Spirit gives us the exact utterances against the enemy;
He becomes our voice and our very word in times of need. Let us
reflect on the life of our Lord Jesus on earth; He spoke to every
situation, just a word changed circumstances. For example, He
turned water into wine, He made the blind to see, He made the
lame to walk, He raised the dead, He cleansed sinners etc. Christ
came and died to give us hope in this hopeless world; He did
not die for angels but for you and me, for all humanity, for those
that will accept Him and live for Him through His Spirit. Christ
overcame the devil through the Word and His blood saying,
"It is written." (Matthew 4:4, 7, 10 NIV); so, let us declare the
same Word against the devil by saying, "It is written..." Speak to
every challenging situation in your life using the Word of God;
quit talking about the situation or complaining about it. Rather
prophesy God's Word in faith to that challenging situation before
you, and see it disappear in the mighty name of Jesus because there
is power in the spoken Word of God!

The outpouring of the Holy Spirit and His leadership is still
the standard that God requires for His children even today and
forever. *God has not changed, and neither are His ways, no matter
the changing of things around us.* Heaven and earth will pass away,
but His Word will never pass away. God's Word is eternal and
stands forever, it changes not, and it is light and life. The Holy
Spirit is the anointing and deposit in our hearts guaranteeing the
Word of the Father and what is to come. We were created for
the glory of God, to worship and adore Him through His Holy
Spirit that is in us. It is the leadership of the Holy Spirit that can

perfect us to be the man or woman the Lord God created us to be. It is only through His power that the minds of people can be changed—from being lovers of themselves and lovers of money, to a powerful men and women of God. However, in this generation, the Holy Spirit is neglected in most churches, out of the lives of many believers, and out of their daily affairs; the leadership of the Holy Spirit is no longer allowed in the worship of God, not even the name of God can be mentioned in our schools and workplaces. What a sad and abominable situation! People have forgotten who they truly are, and whose they are; they have lost their identity, which can only be found in Christ Jesus our Lord. We are sons and daughters of the king of all kings, the owner and creator of the entire universe and everything therein, the giver and sustainer of life, the almighty, and the sovereign one! He has promised that He will never leave us nor forsake us because of His great love towards us; hence He sent His Holy Spirit to be with us forever. Allow the Spirit of the living God to come and dwell in you, and be with you forever in all aspects of your life; you must be born of the Spirit of God as a child of God. Once you start a relationship with Him, you will realize that He is your best friend, your counselor, your healer, your teacher, your helper, your strengthener, your advocate, your intercessor, your comforter, your all and in all. Be fully committed to Him as He speaks to you in that still quiet voice within you, through His Word, fellowship, prayers, dreams, visions, and so on. Let the Holy Spirit be the *first point of contact* in all challenges of your life, and you will enjoy and feed on His faithfulness. *He is the most wonderful person and loving relationship you could ever have in your lifetime, more than anything this world could ever offer you.*

It is the Father's will that we live by His Spirit. His children *must* be of His Spirit, and in the mind of His Spirit. We cannot survive in this life without the Spirit of God because where the Spirit of God is there is freedom from every bondage (2 Corinthians 3:17; Isaiah 61:1–2 NKJV). Whenever a person turns in repentance to the Lord Jesus, the veil of darkness, guilt, and sin, are all stripped off and taken away, and the person becomes a brand-new person born of the Spirit of God. He or she continues to renew their mind to that of Christ's through the Holy Spirit according to God's Word. When the Holy Spirit is in you and at work in you, you will experience the work which His presence within you achieves. These attributes not only show forth the presence of the Holy Spirit in a person but also confirm that he/she is a child of the king: *Love* (the love of God demonstrated in and through you), *joy* (gladness that comes from above and is beyond happiness), *peace* (the peace of God in all circumstances), *patience* (an even temper and forbearance that comes through faith), *kindness* (kind hearted), *goodness* (benevolence in every way that comes through faith), *faithfulness* (being faithful in every way), *gentleness* (is not weakness but meekness and humility), and *self-control* (self-restraint and continence) (Galatians 5:22–23 NKJV). When you live by the Spirit, you walk by the Spirit; meaning that your conduct is controlled by the Spirit of God. It is no more you that lives, no more your ways, or your sinful and carnal desires, but Christ fully lives in you through His Spirit. Christ replaces the pronouns "I" and "We;" His Spirit in you only desires the things that are pleasing in His sight. God moves through His Spirit, which is the life of Christ that comes upon one when he/she repents of his sins, accepts the Lord Jesus as their Lord, and baptizes in the name of Jesus Christ our Lord. The Holy Spirit fills a believer with the power, counsel, wisdom, understanding, knowledge, and reverential fear of the Lord. He brings Christ alive in you by filling you with the love of God, which enables you to love others even in the darkest of times. When the Spirit of the Lord is upon you, you will no longer be ashamed of the Word of God or the gospel, which gives you boldness and revelation that His Word is the power of God unto salvation to anyone that believes. You will then begin to declare what you want to see happen; knowing fully well that there is power in the spoken Word of God.

Those that belong to the Lord Jesus and filled with the presence of the Holy Spirit have crucified their flesh (their godless human nature) with its passions, appetites, and desires. These fleshly desires and practices that include, sexual immorality, impurity, indecency or debauchery, idolatry, sorcery or witchcraft, enmity or hatred, strife or discord, jealousy, anger, selfishness, division or dissensions, heresies or party spirit, envy, drunkenness and carousing, or orgies were all nailed to the cross and dead with Christ (Galatians 5:19–21 NIV); and those who do such things cannot inherit the kingdom of God. So, if you say you are a child of God and live by the Spirit, your life must reflect the presence of the Spirit of Christ within you. This way our Father will be glorified in heaven through the aroma of His love in you and to others; you will not become vain and self-conceited, competitive, challenging, provoking, irritating to others, envying, and jealous of one another. Rather, you will be responsive to, controlled by, and guided by the Holy Spirit of God within you. Thus, you will only desire the things of the Spirit, the things that will bring praise to the Lord God almighty through the power of the Holy Spirit in you. The Holy Spirit in you will bring to pass every spoken Word of God according to your faith, to the glory of our Lord Jesus Christ, the one and only true God; be glory, honor, and power forever and ever! Amen!

CONCLUSION OF THE WHOLE MATTER

Every Word of God stands forever, and never fails! From generation to generation, it endures. Whatever God says in His Word, that settles it; His Word is unchanging and powerful, it resolves every doubt and unbelief. Know and believe that the Lord God exists and that He is a faithful rewarder of them that earnestly seek Him, fear Him, abide in Him, and keep His commandments. When you have a true spiritual relationship with the Lord Jesus, and allow the leadership of His Holy Spirit in your life, you will enjoy your walk with Him in faith. So, activate that living faith in you because without faith, we cannot see nor please God. God's living Word is true and most powerful; tried, tested, and purified in every way since time began. Every spoken or written Word of God has already happened or else it would not be God's Word, since no Word of God has *never* failed and will *never* fail. Our faith in God, in His Word, in what He has done, and in His Holy Spirit, will move any mountain (challenge) in our lives, in the mighty name of Jesus Christ. Fear the Lord God with a reverential fear because He is our creator, the almighty, and omnipotent God, the maker of all things, the supreme, the giver and keeper of life, the invisible, the immortal, the king eternal, the only true God, and to Him be all the glory, honor, majesty, and power forever and ever. Amen! The Lord God is from above and above all things, His ways are higher than our ways, and His thoughts higher than our thoughts. If you love the Lord Jesus

Christ, then do His will; believe in every word that He has said because He is *faithful* and *true* to bring to pass every Word of God declared. God created us and not we ourselves, to have a true relationship with Him, to worship Him, and to proclaim His praise; He made us out of the abundance of His love for us. We are God's, the sheep of His pasture, and we belong to Him. Our entire duty or reason for being here on this planet earth is to praise and worship the Father, and to have a true spiritual relationship with the living God through Christ Jesus. So, align yourself with the unchanging and powerful Word of God, and believe in the Lord Jesus and His Holy Spirit. Declare what the Word of God says in every circumstance you face, and do not agree with the enemy by declaring negative things into your life.

Jesus Christ is the answer for today, the answer to every problem; He is the light of the world. Christ is *all* that we would ever need! He is our identity and blueprint, and in Him lies all our God-given potential. The Holy Spirit is fundamental in our relationship and work with God; we cannot do anything without the Spirit of God; His leadership is the pattern God has set for His children since the birth of Christianity. Hence, there is *no* true Christianity without the Holy Spirit; without the Holy Spirit, our worship of God becomes nothing but mere dead worship devoid of any power or presence of God. It is the Holy Spirit that fills our hearts with the love of God, and this love compels us to worship the Lord God. The love of Christ in us ushers us to worship the Lord because of who God is. As children of God, we must have and be led by the Holy Spirit of God. The Lord longs for a spiritual relationship, and that is all that He desires; a longing heart for Him, a heart of love that pursues after Him. The Father is not interested in man-made programs, teachings, creeds, or deeds, but He is after obedient hearts and souls; the Lord is after a genuine relationship with His people. Change the way you think and speak; have the mind of Christ Jesus through the power of His

Holy Spirit. Renew your mind with God's Word, and make Him the Lord over your entire life today; tomorrow might be too late.

Let us stand firm as children of God, putting on the entire covering of God including but not limited to the Word, faith, His name, and His Holy Spirit. With such in place, we will be able to overcome the evil works of the enemy because there is supernatural power in the spoken Word of God! Be encouraged to feed on God's Word, have faith in Him, trust in Him, and commit to a relationship with the Lord Jesus Christ through His Holy Spirit. It is the Word of God through faith in the Holy Spirit that should rule God's children. God dwells in His Word and speaks by the Word to reveal His will because His Word is His will. Now, let the weak say "I am strong!" let the poor say "I am rich! "and let the sick say "I am healed!" because of what the Lord has done! Arise and shine child of God, child of the most high God, for your light has come, and the glory of the Lord rises upon you in faith! The day is subjected to you, it belongs to you; you oversee the day; so, declare the unchanging and powerful Word of God into your day!

May this Word of God be sown into your heart and soul, and may it grow and bring forth fruits that will last unto eternity, to the glory, honor, and power of the Lord God almighty. May your life, relationship, and walk with the Lord Jesus Christ never be the same again, but grow from glory to glory through the power of His Holy Spirit. And may your work in the Lord continue to be produced by your faith, your labor in Him be encouraged by God's everlasting love, and your endurance in the will of God for your life be inspired by your hope in the Lord Jesus Christ. Finally, may your knowledge and understanding of Christ Jesus be enlightened more and more each day, in His mighty name. Amen! Stay blessed!